The Radical Realism of

Jesus

A Framework for Living in the 21st Century

The Radical Realism of

Jesus

A Framework for Living in the 21st Century

Jeyran Main

Review Tales Publishing & Editing Services

Review Tales

The Radical Realism of Jesus: A Framework for Living in the 21st Century
© 2025 by Jeyran Main

Published in the United States of America by Review Tales Publishing & Editing Services. This book may be purchased in bulk for educational, business, fundraising, or promotional use. For information, please email: Jeyran.main@gmail.com
All Scripture quotations in this book, unless otherwise noted, are taken from the New King James Version (NKJV).

ISBN (Hardcover): 978-1-988680-89-7
ISBN (Paperback): 978-1-988680-88-0
ISBN (Digital): 978-1-988680-87-3

The information in this book is intended for devotional, inspirational, and educational purposes only.
Printed in the United States of America

To my father, whose guidance and wisdom set me on this path and shaped the purpose of this book.

To Zakaria, Elijah, and Amina, whose curiosity, love, and joy remind me daily of the wonder in learning, questioning, and seeking truth. May this work honor the values you inspire in me.

"In Him was life, and that life was the light of men. And the light shines in the darkness, and the darkness did not comprehend it."

- John 1:4–5

Acknowledgments

I am indebted to the thinkers whose work informed this book. The writings of Thomas Aquinas, Blaise Pascal, Søren Kierkegaard, Karl Barth, Paul Tillich, C.S. Lewis, N.T. Wright, Alister McGrath, John Polkinghorne, Charles Taylor, William Lane Craig, and James K.A. Smith provided both intellectual depth and critical perspective. Their ideas challenged me to wrestle with reason, faith, history, and ethics in new ways, and their voices echo throughout the chapters that follow.

I also wish to acknowledge the many other scholars—through writings, lectures, and sermons—who have shaped my understanding of Scripture and theology. Their intellectual rigor offered a framework that informed the ideas presented here.

A heartfelt thank you goes to the community at Maple City Church. Your warmth, support, and willingness to engage with my questions made this journey both possible and joyful. Your friendship and encouragement were invaluable as I worked to articulate these thoughts.

I am especially grateful to Pastors Rick Dressler, Dan Christiaans, and Andrew McCombe. Over the years, your patients' answers to my questions, thoughtful guidance through Bible studies, and encouragement in times of doubt have been immeasurable. I am equally grateful to Effie Gabriel, whose generosity in sharing wisdom—even when I pressed for clarity—helped me navigate complex ideas and strengthened my understanding of Scripture and theology.

I am deeply grateful to my father, whose guidance and encouragement helped me discern the direction and purpose of this book. Your wisdom and support have been foundational to this work.

Finally, I extend my thanks to the readers who will engage with this book. It is my hope that this exploration of Jesus in dialogue with modern thought will challenge, inspire, and invite reflection.

To all of you, I offer my deepest gratitude.

Table of Contents

PREFACE

In our modern world, shaped by science, technology, and rapidly evolving ideas, it can be challenging to see how the life and teachings of Jesus remain relevant. This book was written to offer a perspective on Christ that is not distant or abstract, but alive — capable of speaking into the complexities of contemporary life, the questions we wrestle with, and the assumptions we often take for granted. My hope is that readers will approach these pages with openness, curiosity, and a willingness to see how Jesus continues to unsettle, challenge, and inspire. The Gospels repeatedly show us that Jesus does not fit into neat categories; he disrupted the religious systems of his day, overturned tradition, and challenged people's assumptions about God, life, and themselves. This disruptive reality echoes Kierkegaard's insistence that to encounter Christ is an existential confrontation that interrupts expectations and requires a suspension of disbelief (Kierkegaard 1843). Karl Barth likewise notes that Jesus is not an abstraction to be tamed by human thought but is the living Word that confronts and modifies our understanding of God and the world (Barth 1932–1968).

Yet we exist now, in the twenty-first century, in a very dissimilar world. Our societies have been shaped by two great revolutions: the scientific Renaissance and the Industrial Revolution. What emerged from those revolutions were whole new visions of living—rationalism, empiricism, scientism, pragmatism, and even nihilism. Each of these perspectives has promised insight and control, but often leaves us with more questions than answers. Alister McGrath argues that scientific and empirical frameworks were strikingly adept at answering "how," but do poorly at answering a "why" (McGrath 2015). Charles Taylor also notes that, while modern secularism can still produce a feeling of meaninglessness, human beings still desire transcendence (Taylor 2007). In a society ruled by data, algorithms, and material progress, Jesus can feel like a historical abstraction from an idealized past. Christianity can be dismissed, along with other faiths, as idealism, and is tightly bound by the realism of modern life. However, John Polkinghorne's work demonstrates that faith does not have to conflict with science; Jesus is not irrelevant even in a world governed by logic, mathematics, and the laws of physics (Polkinghorne 1989).

However, this book is written by a different conviction: that the words of Jesus revealed in Scripture are not abstractions or an old ideal. Pascal wrote centuries ago that reason cannot answer the most fundamental questions of the heart and existence (Pascal 1670). William Lane Craig presents similar evidence, suggesting that empirical or rational systems cannot adequately describe moral, existential, or metaphysical realities that are not rationally comprehensible (Craig 2008). Your engagement with Jesus must grapple with the boundaries of these philosophies, while also borrowing from the insights of each. Realism, pragmatism, and rationalism may inform your understanding of the world. Still, none of these philosophies can provide an understanding of the fullness of life, the restoration of the heart, or the reconciliation of the soul.

The gospel continues to challenge us because it will never be fully contained within any human system. Grace is not as rational as we desire it to be. Mercy is not pragmatic in the worldly sense. Forgiveness often feels irrational or even impossible. Yet it is precisely in this tension—between our current frameworks and the radical words of Christ—that real life can be found. N. T. Wright reminds us that we need to read Jesus against his own historical and cultural context, exposing a Kingdom that upends ancient and contemporary assumptions (Wright 1996). Paul Tillich positions Christ as the ultimate existential answer, merging theology with human lived experience (Tillich 1951). C. S. Lewis demonstrates that the gracious moral and spiritual insights of Christ can still be useful and meaningful to life, and to some extent even more so, in the twenty-first century (Lewis 1952).

This book wants to read the Gospels with this intention. We will not simply peruse the historical and cultural words of Jesus as we would examine some remarkable yet distant museum pieces. We are going to delve into living words that pierce through the mindsets of the first century and the assumptions of the twenty-first century! We will consider how Christ speaks to a rationalist who is obsessed with logic, to an empiricist who is only capable of trusting what can be measured, to a pragmatist who is only trying to figure out what works, to, no kidding, a nihilist who isn't even sure that meaning exists in life! Each chapter will explore how the Kingdom of God interrupts, contradicts, and fulfills philosophies that shape and influence cultural life today.

Matthew shows us that genuine righteousness extends beyond rules. Mark depicts a suffering King whose victory redefines triumph. Luke reminds us that power is reversed in God's economy. John depicts an eternal Word, the Logos, who provides meaning and life itself. And Paul tells us that we are being remade in the image of Christ—not by our achievement, but by grace (Rom. 8:29).

At the heart of this book is realism: the realism of Jesus. Not idealism or abstract spirituality, but a real, lived-out faith which confronts our doubts, our science, our technology, and our modern anxieties with the very same grace that astonished tax collectors and lifelong Pharisees two thousand years ago. Jesus unsettled the assumptions of his time, and he continues to unsettle our assumptions today. And if we are willing, he will unsettle our assumptions, too—not to demolish, but to offer us a new heart, a new spirit, and a new way of being human in the very world that we actually live in today.

INTRODUCTION
JESUS WILL NOT BE DOMESTICATED

*f*rom the beginning, Jesus has consistently defied human expectations. As Dane Ortlund puts it, Christ is uncooperative with the neat and tidy boxes that humans want him to fit into. A close reading of the Gospels clearly demonstrates that Jesus defied societal conventions. He clashed with the Pharisees, acted out against religious customs, attempted not to be intimidated by Roman officials, and even confronted the expectations of His own disciples (Matthew 23; Luke 11). This is an existential idea that Kierkegaard emphasized: faith is a tension-filled encounter with the paradoxical and unpredictable claim of God (Fear and Trembling, 1843). Karl Barth emphasizes that Jesus does not allow us to tame Him by our definitions; He is the living Word who confronts our assertions and reformulates our ideas of God and our world (Church Dogmatics, 1932-1968).

In the 21st century, we have lived through a revolution of intellectual conceptions and witnessed revolutionary technological advancements. The Scientific Revolution led to the acceptance of empirical reasoning, systematic observations, and rational investigation as aspirational conceptions of understanding. The Industrial Revolution transformed human society through the mechanization of all aspects of human life, urbanization, and the creation of a modern economy. Today, digital and technological revolutions are pushing further into reconstructing knowledge, social interactions, and human priorities. These revolutions have redefined our understanding of reality, giving rise to worldviews such as Realism, Rationalism, Pragmatism, Empiricism, Scientism, and Nihilism. Alister McGrath notes that this claim has led to significant progress in formulating "how" questions; however, it fails to fulfill the more basic human desire for meaning (The Big Question, 2015). Charles Taylor's discussion of secularism and modern rationality similarly suggests that secularism and modern rationality can lead human beings to feel cast adrift, a sense of loss of transcendence amidst material advances (A Secular Age, 2007).

This book examines Jesus in the context of these modern frameworks. In contrast to situating Jesus as either a timeless ideal or a simple allegory, we view Jesus as a historical figure who engages with contemporary philosophies through his life, teachings, and ministry.

Christianity is incarnational, in that God stepped into time, space, and history as a totally embodied human being in Jesus. John Polkinghorne argues that beings literate enough to think scientifically, with the appropriate epistemic humility, don't need to compartmentalize logic, reason, or faith in a natural world explained by a priori reasoning (Science and Providence, 1989). Jesus remains aspirational, even in a world where human existence is subject to measurement and empirical laws govern life. Jesus is the "Word became flesh and dwelt among us" (John 1:14). Jesus did not pontificate from an ivory tower, but engaged with experiences of hunger, fatigue, moral dilemmas, betrayal, and hope — a type of realism that takes on ancient and modern paradigms of what is possible for humans. In a manner similar to Pascal, the heart has questions that cannot be answered by rationality alone (Pensées, 1670). William Lane Craig would argue that systems of understanding based purely on rational and/or empirical grounds fail to interrogate moral or existential truths (Reasonable Faith, 2008).

In this light, the book aims to assess the thought frames that dominate contemporary thought, presenting Jesus as competent for engagement with intellect, ethics, and spirituality. It is evident that N.T. Wright articulates that the historical Jesus must be understood in the context of revealing a kingdom that transcends all ancient structures and modern presumptions (Jesus and the Victory of God, 1996). Paul Tillich presents Christ as an existential response to human questions, offering a narrative that bridges theology and experience (Systematic Theology, 1951). C.S. Lewis reminds us that Christ's moral and spiritual teachings remain salient across time and place (Mere Christianity, 1952). Each chapter will examine Jesus' life and teachings through a particular set of assumptions or lenses, including Realism, Rationalism, Empiricism, Pragmatism, Scientism, and Nihilism. The intention is not to preach, but to wrestle, reflect, and demonstrate that the Gospel remains disruptive, challenging, and transformative--much like it disrupted, challenged, and transformed a people two thousand years ago.

The Kingdom of God is not abstract or domesticated. It is concrete, relational, and supra-rational--an engagement with reason, ethics, history, and lived experience. Jesus still demands thought, reflection, and action. The book seeks to engage with the life of Jesus, considering the questions, skepticism, and ethical issues that arise when engaging with the Gospel in a modern era.

ENGAGING THE GREAT CONVERSATION

*P*lacing Jesus in the mix of a broader conversation helps us see Jesus not merely as an abstract ideal, but as a tangible, historical, embodied, and relational reality—a person. For several hundred years, thinkers from various epochs, locations, and perspectives—classical theology and philosophy; modern and contemporary philosophers, theologians, and Christian educators; engagement with the historical-critical study of scripture; and engagement with science, to name a few—have wrestled with perennial human questions of truth, meaning, ethics, and encounter with the divine and with each other. While they engage questions through distinct methodologies and cultural contexts, there is a shared pursuit of human knowledge, uncertainty of reason, and the encounter with something divine. A number of these thinkers describe how Jesus—his life, teachings, and relations—transcends centuries to remain important concerning ethical reflection, social, relational and historical accountability, and existential transformation (Aquinas 1947; Craig 2008; Lewis 1952;

Pascal 1966; Polkinghorne 2001; Sanders 1993; Smith 2014; Taylor 2007; Wright 1996; Vermes 1973).

These thinkers offer a range of perspectives through which we can consider Jesus. Classical thinkers emphasize reason, metaphysics, and moral order—for instance, the way human inquiry positions itself in relation to the divine and the incarnation (Aquinas 1947; Pascal 1966). Modern and contemporary thinkers engage with existential, cultural, and scientific realities to respond to skepticism, pluralism, and moral uncertainty, providing contemporary relevance to what Jesus means for us today (Craig 2008; Taylor 2007; Smith 2014; McGrath 2000; Polkinghorne 2001). The historical Jesus, as an avenue of research, uses critical methods and critical contextualization of Jesus' ministry and life, affirming an understanding of the human reality of Jesus—acknowledging that engagement isn't merely theoretical or devotional, but historically and ethically informed (Sanders 1993; Crossan 1991; Wright 1996; Vermes 1973).

Identifying thinkers who highlight unique dimensions that provide opportunities for responding to attempts to discuss Jesus are complementary and worthy of engagement. While one thinker may emphasize the rational, historical, or scientific dimensions of understanding Jesus, another will foreground the relational, existential, or ethical commitments. In this manner, these conversations in the aggregate provide essential contours for thinking about Jesus as a radical realist—historically verifiable, ethically important, relationally present, and transcendent (Aquinas 1947; Craig 2008; Lewis 1952; Pascal 1966; Polkinghorne 2001; Sanders 1993; Smith 2014; Taylor 2007; Wright 1996; Vermes 1973).

In framing this larger conversation (to think of Jesus not as an abstract ideal or theory), it positions the reader to engage with Jesus as a human, as a living being, whose life and teachings connect to human reason, culture, ethics, and relationships. Establishing these conceptual foundations situates this text and Jesus as relevant, transformative, and essential for faith, thought, and human flourishing in the twenty-first century.

Classical and Pre-Modern Foundations

In the foundational writing of Thomas Aquinas titled Summa Theologica (Aquinas 1947), he emphasizes the connection between reason and faith. Therefore, truths established through the empirical inquiry of natural philosophy indicate God to be the source of those happenings. The Logos, according to Aquinas, is more than an abstract idea; divine truth is knowable by human reasoning and must point to something ontologically existent. From this perspective, it is therefore accurate to say that the incarnation of Jesus is not an abstract thought, but the embodiment of rational and moral ordering, while simultaneously being a bridge between the human logos and the figured. Reasoned inquiry by Aquinas is, then, not in contradiction with faith but may in fact prepare the rational mind to specifically orient itself towards Jesus by virtue of its lived, historical, and moral form of engagement (Aquinas 1947). Aquinas not only insists that ethical reflection, moral reasoning, and metaphysical inquiry are not unrelated to divine truths, but they also function as conduits to understanding how Jesus exhibits the fulfillment of God's ultimate purposes throughout human history. In this light, the intellectual and spiritual aspects of Aquinas's thought are fundamentally integrated, providing a framework for approaching Jesus as a historical and rationally encountered figure. Thus, the pre-modern thought of Aquinas encourages ontology and metaphysics through a disciplined reflection that ethically situates a rational inquiry into history, converging to uncover the reality of Jesus of Nazareth as an ontologically human and fully divine agent.

Pascal, writing in Pensées (Pascal 1966, 71), confronts the skepticism and rationalism of modernity as reflective of existential propositions. He notes that reason cannot explicate the longings of the human heart and the divine engagement of experience, where he states, "the heart has its reasons which reason knows nothing of." Pascal's comments tend to draw attention to the tensions of modernity: empirical or reasoned inquiry may reveal the world and/or God in reflective matters, but only the relational reality of Jesus, an actual historical person, may ground existential engagement whatsoever. Pascal goes on to emphasize that faith is not simply an intellectual position but a lived experience or encounter, highlighting the relational aspect of Christianity. While Aquinas emphasizes systematic reason as a basis for ethical and spiritual belief, Pascal emphasizes the experiential, affective, and relational aspects through which human beings understand the divine. To bring the perspective of both Aquinas and Pascal, the reader is urged to engage with Jesus as both knowable through reason and known through relational lived experience, effectively bridging abstract thought with existential reality (Pascal 1966).

These pre-modern authors collectively endorse both the primarily dualistic approaches to Jesus as both intelligible and historically existent, and simultaneously transformative, existential beings. Their frameworks do not treat the Gospel as a mythologized abstraction but conjoin claims through reasoned inquiry, historical engagement, and human experience. Aquinas provides the rational and moral scaffolding to support a belief. At the same time, Pascal offers engagement and lived, relational aspects that bring the believer into a deeper relationship with the incarnate Christ. They are creating a thorough foundation for knowing Jesus as historically arranged, morally significant, and existentially transformational in a way that is accessible to evangelicals who have both rational and relational responses to Christ, rather than proposing the conscious, abstract, or rational thought found in modernity.

Existential and Modern Theology

In *Fear and Trembling* and *The Concept of Anxiety*, Søren Kierkegaard consistently argues that our authentic engagement with Christ is either existentially distinct or nonexistent (Kierkegaard 1983). Kierkegaard argues that faith is not a commitment to certain propositions (about God, Jesus, Christianity, and how to live), but instead, faith is our engagement with an ethical and spiritual reality (Kierkegaard 1983). Søren Kierkegaard's concern for the subjectivity of individual engagement with reality resonates with contemporary readers navigating a tension between abstract and real ideas. However, this tension is not as catastrophic as Kierkegaard draws it, as he often draws the so-called leap of faith as more important than a historically unpleasant grounding. This book, however, emphasizes that our encounter with Jesus must always be set within real events—that is, Christ's life, death, and resurrection—as they are recounted in the Gospels (Kierkegaard 1983).

Karl Barth, in *Church Dogmatics*, reads Jesus as the living Word that confronts contemporary thought; he does not make theological and secret moves towards the alternatives offered by contemporary cultural and philosophical positions; he only expresses the theological reality in dialogue (Barth 1967). Barth insists that revelation stands above abstract speculation and that Jesus addresses real human issues in real time, not idealized moral events for us to think about abstractly. So Barth's thematic inquiry aligns with my emphasis on embodied realism; to him, Jesus was a real person, a historical figure, who, in light of who Jesus was and is, makes ethical claims upon community life (Barth 1967). So, suppose respect for Jesus is primarily about historical works, first-century Jewish ethics, actions, and human agency. In that case, Jesus in the New Testament confronts the constructs and presuppositions of first-century Judea, as well as the contemporary expressions of these ideas in the modern world (Barth 1967).

Paul Tillich, in *Systematic Theology*, synthesizes the spheres of existential philosophy and Christian theology, arguing that ultimate concern is the central point of understanding meaning in human life (Tillich 1967). In doing so, he is aware of how objection has become process and proposes that ultimate reality can only be articulated on the level of relationality, which consists of what is often regarded, in popular terms, as intellectual engagement (Tillich 1967). Indeed, while it could be understood that Tillich is bringing together existential angst with theological understanding, as Kierkegaard and Barth had also noted, his notion of ultimate concern sustains a consideration as a system of inquiry, analysing how Jesus negotiates modern human issues meaningfully regarding identity and human anxiety, and, importantly, moral responsibility, without as he diminish it completely to abstraction (Tillich 1967).

All together, these existential and modern theologians illustrate a need for engaging Jesus existentially as a figure of only pertinence to us, but also as one who carries any weight in our historical understanding. While none of these writers stand on the whole of existentialism (Kierkegaard subjective individual; Barth divinely confronted Jesus and as faced by the human condition; Tillich existential synthesis), they join the overarching claim wrought by them all; Jesus' life, his teaching, and who or how Jesus is to their own sense of presence cannot be relegated to ideology or abstract/intellectualism.

Engaging Science, Philosophy, and Secular Culture

The writings of C.S. Lewis, in both *Mere Christianity* and *The Abolition of Man*, incorporate both secular rationalism and a moral philosophy aimed at achieving imaginative clarity (Lewis 1952, 32; Lewis 1947, 15). Lewis proposed that reason and moral law could inform a transcendence. Lewis demonstrates that human reasoning, while powerful, cannot exist in a vacuum of ethical consideration—reason is not enough for a complete apprehension of reality, morality, and God. Lewis situates Jesus at the point of convergence for ethics, human desire, and rational reflection, suggesting that the incarnate Christ provides a framework within which human development of thought, moral deliberation, and existential inquiry can coexist. In confronting the skepticism inherent to the modern age, Lewis demonstrates that reason and morality, properly oriented, can point beyond themselves to the concrete person of Jesus. Lewis's efforts bridge the divide between intellectual rigor and spiritual experience, in which faith is neither irrational nor discrete from reason, but is finding its complement within reason. This qualified faith positions Jesus not only as a moral teacher, but a point of intersection for ethical insights and rational thought (Lewis 1952, 32; Lewis 1947, 15).

N.T. Wright's scholarship, particularly *Jesus and the Victory of God*, situates the historical Jesus within the context of his first-century life in first-century Judea (Wright 1996, 45). Wright grounds the historical Jesus in the socio-political and religious realities of first-century Palestine, and observes that serious engagements with Jesus must mean considering Jesus in those specific circumstances. Wright observes that modern readers tend to abstract Jesus in terms of ideals, ethical generalizations, or myth. Wright observes that, regardless of how readers engage with the text, Jesus was a historical person in a specific place and time. Wright's anthropological approach, which roots Jesus' lived reality in contextual readings of first-century Jewish life, political situation, and theological orientations, demonstrates that Jesus' teachings and actions emerge grounded in those lived realities rather than theoretical engagements. Historical engagement does not lessen the theological engagement with Jesus. Instead, it affirms the integrity of considering the ethical, relational, and redemptive contexts of Jesus' life, teaching, and living (Wright 1996, 45). By engaging with the lived context of Jesus, Wright reminds us that faith is grounded in historical reality and does not require the abandonment of ethical insight, relational understanding, or redemptive engagement.

Alister McGrath's *Science & Religion* offers a model for engaging with scientific thought while maintaining theological clarity (McGrath 2000, 78). McGrath engages with the tensions perceived between empirical investigation and religious beliefs, and how claims about Jesus' life intersect with both the natural world and moral reasoning. He offers a critique of reductionist materialism and scientism, showing that faith does not preclude some engagement with science. John Polkinghorne, in parallel, explores the Christian engagement with science and the implications for theology within *Science and Providence* (Polkinghorne 2001, 92). Polkinghorne demonstrates the importance of examining the natural order and divine action as mutually existing and therefore mutually informing. Both McGrath and Polkinghorne demonstrate how Jesus' historical life illustrates a model through which rational, empirical, and ethical forms of knowledge triangulate, yielding a coherent and multidimensional understanding of reality (McGrath 2000, 78; Polkinghorne 2001, 92). Together, these thinkers show us that engaging with science and philosophy in secular culture and society does not weaken the historicity, ethical significance, and spiritual force of Jesus' life, but instead points toward a realization to which the work of faith, reason, and observation can stir the heart and mind.

Philosophical Engagement with Modernity

The contemporary landscape of philosophy provides a rich conversation partner for reflecting on the place of Jesus in today's world. Charles Taylor, in *A Secular Age*, provides a comprehensive understanding of the social and intellectual contexts that enabled the emergence of secular modernity (Taylor 2007). Taylor tracks how the movement from a world where all was religious to one where belief is now optional has given rise to new conceptions of meaning and identity, and more recently, the moral landscape. Taylor's analysis illustrates the cultural task that Jesus faces today. In our connected world, he is now contending with minds and hearts shaped by pluralism, rationalization, and immanence over transcendence (Taylor 2007). Acknowledging these concerns, Jesus' teaching is a coherent moral and relational vision. If a robust cultural scaffolding of faith is absent, aspects of this vision can still hold meaning for people today.

William Lane Craig perceives modernity through a different, though no less robust, lens. Craig's apologia for the philosophy of modernity, *Reasonable Faith*, offers engaging ideas about scientism, nihilism, and naturalism. Using classical and analytic philosophy, Craig argues, among other things, for a historical and metaphysical resurrection of Jesus. In this book and elsewhere, Craig demonstrates that rational bases for belief are possible, even with empirical verification, and the logic of skepticism permeates a culture (Craig 2008). This book's approach is systematic and apologetic. In contrast, a relational and ethical witness rooted in historical context demonstrates that the Jesus of history, ethics, and relationships is not a claim that simply verifies Jesus' existence.

In *How (Not) to Be Secular*, James K.A. Smith demonstrates the formative role of habits, cultural rhythms, and pre-reflective action in shaping beliefs (Smith 2014). For Smith, rationality is one component of faith, but regular practices, human desires, and habits pointing to ultimate ends form beliefs over time (Smith 2014). Smith's ideas are representative of the incarnational approach of this book. Jesus literally comes into life and shapes discipleship through ordinary work, family, and social rhythms that are relationally oriented, practical, and transformatively historical in context.

Alister McGrath, in *Science & Religion: An Introduction*, combines theology, science, and culture to show that empirical inquiry and Christian faith can coexist in cases of unlikely indistinctness and exclusion (McGrath 2011). John Polkinghorne, in *Science and Providence*, similarly argues that what we call natural law can form or cohere spiritual realities as a collective aesthetic, contributing to an integrated understanding of creation (Polkinghorne 2005). These thinkers, and others like them, validate the project of this book. We engaged scientifically literate and philosophically critical readers with the conclusion about Jesus as historical, ethical, and relationally real.

By examining the work of Taylor, Craig, Smith, McGrath, and Polkinghorne, we see that modernity offers considerable criticism on identity, morality, and human limitation, but has difficulty improving relationality, history, and meaning that is, or is ascribed as, transcendent. Jesus' historical, ethical, and relational claims—his birth, ministry, and resurrection—can counter secular decay coherently, because they enable contemporary readers to think about ethics, culture, and reason without relegating life to concepts divorced from history, morality, or empirical tropes (Taylor 2007; Craig 2008; Smith 2014; McGrath 2011; Polkinghorne 2005).

Historical Jesus Scholars Relevant to Modern Engagement

The field of historical Jesus studies equips scholars with valuable resources for contextualizing Jesus as a real, particular, and historically grounded figure who remains equally relevant to today's audience. E. P. Sanders, in *The Historical Figure of Jesus* (1993), organizes Jesus' first-century Jewish context and examines his actions, teachings, and historical location. Sanders demonstrates how, in contemporary reading, it is possible to have both an empirical reading of Jesus and a historically literate reading that is consistent with the ethical and spiritual changes Jesus' ministry brought about (Sanders 1993). Sanders discloses the particular socio-historical context of Jesus. With this, it is possible to counter secular interpretations that reduce Jesus to a myth or a moral ideal and see that Jesus' life bears historical meaning and ethical weight.

John Dominic Crossan, in *The Historical Jesus* (1991), offers a historical reading of Jesus, considering the social, political, and religious context in which Jesus lived. His inductive approach is evidence-based, not devotional, which allows a modern readership—even if they reject traditional religious claims—to see Jesus as a real, active, historically situated person (Crossan 1991). Crossan maintains a serious focus on the ethical challenges that Jesus posed to social and religious systems, which allows modern audiences to consider the significance of Jesus' re-envisioning in a pluralistic, critical context.

N. T. Wright, in *Jesus and the Victory of God* (1996), provides a historical reading—also framed as a theological interpretation—by considering Jesus as the culmination of God's covenantal promises in a decisive act in history for the inauguration of the Kingdom of God (Wright 1996). Furthermore, Wright's scholarship demonstrates that Jesus' ministry and life were historically verifiable and spiritually profound, yet faithfully ethical, thus aligning well with a rendering that emphasizes the relational dimensions of historical fact and theological meaning.

Geza Vermes, especially in *Jesus the Jew* (1973), draws on Jewish traditions to acknowledge the continuity Jesus had with these ethical and spiritual frameworks, even as he radically sought to renew them as part of the culture in which he was a part (Vermes 1973). By giving attention to Jesus' overlap with and challenge to first-century Judaism, Vermes highlights that Jesus as a historical character has an ethical potentiality as a revolutionary figure, historically framed.

Altogether, the scholarly work of Sanders, Crossan, Wright, and Vermes establishes a firm historical foundation for the developments presented in this book. In portraying Jesus as a real, incarnational figure, his life, teachings, and ongoing social implications—as historically, ethically, and spiritually related—offer informative insights into his relevance to modern subject matter, situating him between historical academics and present-day, contemporary engagement (Sanders 1993; Crossan 1991; Wright 1996; Vermes 1973).

Integrating Insights: Where These Thinkers Meet the Book

Throughout the centuries, these thinkers, as a collective, have paved pathways for us to engage with Jesus. They engage Jesus with reason, history, ethics, and relational depth. The pre-modern theologians are more than philosophers and thinkers—Aquinas and Pascal provide us with historic traditions that are rich enough to showcase how faith is not opposed to reason but aligns with a coherent articulation. For example, Aquinas shows us how the gifts we might call precepts of natural law, ethos as it manifests in ethics, and that we might even license as a metaphysical or rational reasoning, provide an enactment of knowledge based on a common experience, some might call God, and others humanity (Aquinas 1947). These are meaningful ways to engage rational inquiry and self-identify that Christ is real. In contrast, Pascal shows us that human reason alone is insufficient to help us understand the exigent and relational nature of faith. Yet, this encapsulation requires a personal encounter and trust in God as an implicit assembling of unencumbered trust (Pascal 1966).

Theological conversations advanced with the influence of modern theologians, who integrated theology with the notions articulated by Kierkegaard, Barth, and Tillich. It is not only that Jesus was a historical figure; He is also existentially significant. Kierkegaard invites the reader to acknowledge that they are not only responsible for their commitments but also responsible and able to confront the paradoxes of pursuing a Christ-like being within themselves (Kierkegaard 1983). Barth views Jesus as the only significant figure who asserts the claims of revelation and a knowable encounter with God, made real through Jesus (Barth 1967). Tillich writes from an existential perspective and makes it explicit that Jesus speaks meaningfully. He does so by addressing ultimate concerns, now more generally identified as fear, anxiety, and a hunger for a meaningful framework (Tillich 1967). This has a connection to our theology, even if it is fixed in a more secular world than it seems operational within:

It is as if contemporary philosophers and cultural scholars, such as Charles Taylor, James K.A. Smith, Alister McGrath, and John Polkinghorne, look at Jesus, enabling modern readers to navigate socially complex, scientifically fragmented, and culturally disorienting ways in which they can more readily engage with Jesus. Taylor and Smith encourage the idea that belief develops as a result of culturally shaping, rhythmic, and habitual patterns of being habitually connected in social relations (Taylor 2007; Smith 2014). McGrath and Polkinghorne further develop this idea by considering how science informs faith in specific ways, as complementary and inclusive rather than exclusive (McGrath 2011; Polkinghorne 2005). William Lane Craig builds the rational apologetic component to their insights. He suggests reasons grounded in historical and metaphysical rationality to engage readers who insist on critical thinking, interaction, and the development of a skeptical mind (Craig 2008).

Scholarly interpretations about the historical Jesus engage the reflections of E.P. Sanders, John Dominic Crossan, and N.T. Wright and Geza Vermes, or other historians reflecting on the topic. They all express that it makes sense in the Jewish, political, and social contexts of Jesus' ministry and faith. They take the historical position that Jesus sanctioned, albeit that the contestations and tensions of ethical aspirations are made more real in His substance as an existential phenomenon (Sanders 1993; Crossan 1991; Wright 1996; Vermes 1973). This profound reality checks our perceptions and affords evidence and context for systems in which to let Jesus be present through lived experience.

What we hope and have sought to promote in the current book is that we have helped create a multidimensional encounter for the reader towards become a more informed and engaged scholar of what Jesus, historically available contextually oriented as an involved community member grounded declined and issue the expectations also to see Jesus proportioned relational capacity framed historically knowable context, ethically compelling, intellectually coherent, and relationally transformative. We are not suggesting that faith is a calculated blind leap, but rather that it involves engaging with a known figure whose lived experience and resurrection intersect with reason, evidence, culture, and the human existential experience, operating on both subjective and objective paradigms. Consequently, we summarize being informed in the evaluating circumstances provides sufficient framework combining the ideas provided by the noted thinkers; Jesus is about the historical, ethical, and transcendent as existential and that Jesus has something principally meaningful to say to a modern or living context (Aquinas 1947; Pascal 1966; Kierkegaard 1983; Barth 1967; Tillich 1967; Taylor 2007; Smith 2014; McGrath 2011; Polkinghorne 2005; Craig 2008; Sanders 1993; Crossan 1991; Wright 1996; Vermes 1973).

Synthesis: Jesus in Dialogue with Modern Thought

The perspectives put forth by these thinkers—and the reason for including their perspectives—exemplify the fullness of human understanding of Jesus as both a historic, ethical, and spiritually compelling figure. Together, they provide a rich layering of views that engage with and shed light on the multifaceted reality of Jesus. For example, both Thomas Aquinas and Blaise Pascal remind the reader that to engage with the truth of God requires both robust reasoning and deep existential contemplation. Aquinas argues that rational inquiry, by its nature, leads to a grammatical understanding of God and thus plays a role in an ordered moral system. Although human reason can reveal to a person the essence of God, it is not antithetical to faith, but rather part of understanding divine truth (Aquinas 1947, 1225–1274). Pascal, on the other hand, acknowledges the limited role of reason and the ultimate necessity of the heart, relational experience, and personal engagement to apprehend the Divine (Pascal 1966, 1623–1662). Both methodologies clearly share the burden of proof. Both philosophers suggest that the desire for God is inherently human, both ethically and existentially; they also affirm that Jesus, as a historical figure, is best understood through empirical and lived experience.

Kierkegaard, Barth, and Tillich further extend this reflection into a contemporary context, demonstrating the relevance of Jesus Christ to the anxieties and moral ambiguities of modernity. Kierkegaard, in particular, emphasizes the requirement of an existential commitment to a personal engagement with the ethical and spiritual dimensions of following Christ (Kierkegaard 1983, 1813–1855). Barth emphasizes the priority of revelation and the historicity of Jesus as the living Word that interrupts human existence (Barth 1967, 1886–1968). Tillich places Jesus within the construct of ultimate concern, demonstrating how theological findings show that theologians are responding to the existentially significant historical realities of fundamental human plight, such as fear, longing, and meaning (Tillich 1967, 1886–1965). Together, these modern theologians demonstrate that Jesus' meaning is not found in some doctrinal ascent, but rather in his confrontation with the existential realities of human life that are entangled in both historical and contemporary realities.

Modern philosophers and cultural thinkers provide helpful tools for thinking about Jesus in secular, scientific, and cultural ways. Taylor and Smith demonstrate how culture imposes its habits, social rhythms, and moral frameworks to shape beliefs, discipleship, and faith (Taylor 2007; Smith 2014). McGrath and Polkinghorne have argued that the rationality of science and empiricism, alongside theological exploration, can form models to think about nature and the divine in complementary ways (McGrath 2000, 2011; Polkinghorne 2005). Craig adds the rational apologetic lens, showing how historical and metaphysical reasoning can actually support the faith dynamic of Jesus, even in a skeptical or empirically driven culture (Craig 2008). Together, these thinkers offer ways to negotiate the intellectual challenges and cultural hurdles of modernity while being committed to the historical, ethical, and relational implications that Jesus' life and teaching imply.

Lastly, the emergent historical Jesus scholarship (E. P. Sanders, John Dominic Crossan, N. T. Wright, and Geza Vermes) anchors this engagement work presumptively in historicity. Historical Jesus writers examine the socio-political and religious contexts of Jesus' life, reminding readers that faith in Jesus is not merely an understanding of a religious idea, but rather an understanding of Jesus that is tied to the ethical relationships and human experience situated in history (Sanders 1993; Crossan 1991; Wright 1996; Vermes 1973). Together, these theological, philosophical, and historical conversations demonstrate that Jesus is both significantly historical and existentially transformative. He is not a myth, but a flesh-and-blood realist, whose life, teachings, and resurrection challenge a modern reader to respond to the implications of reason, ethics, and culture. Engaging with and including these great thinkers demonstrates that thinking about Jesus is rigorous and multidimensional, encapsulated by the historical and cultural implications of observing Jesus. By synthesizing philosophy, theology, and historical scholarship into a narrative, the Engagement Section provides further assurance that the Gospel remains both authentic and relevant.

Toward a Modern Realist Christology

Ultimately, the Engagement Section leaves Jesus situated as the integrative center of our inquiry—historical, ethical, relational, and transcendent. Jesus is not only a person to study in the abstract, but also a person whose life, teachings, and actions intersect with multiple dimensions of human experience. Jesus offers us coherence, moral fineness, and relational depth that is compelling intellectually as well as spiritually formative, regardless of whether we engage with reason, empirical observation, a pragmatism of outcomes, scientific engagement, or existential despair. In the life of Jesus, we have a framework of sorts through which our human questions about meaning, morality, and relationality can be approached in grounded, consistent, and transformative ways.

Classical thinkers, such as Thomas Aquinas and Blaise Pascal, for example, help us see how rational inquiry and existential reflection on divine truth mutually work together in understanding, and validate that faith and reason are not opposed, but rather mutually reinforce one another (Aquinas 1947; Pascal 1966). Modern theologians, such as Kierkegaard, Barth, and Tillich, elucidate how the significance of Jesus exceeds past historical analysis, offering ethical and existential relevance to the anxieties, doubts, and ambiguities of our lived experience here and now in the present (Kierkegaard 1983; Barth 1967; Tillich 1967). Contemporary philosophers and cultural thinkers, Charles Taylor, James K.A. Smith, Alister McGrath, John Polkinghorne, and William Lane Craig, provide contemporary analytical and scientific frameworks to envision Jesus as the radical realist, pondering but not simply abstracting Jesus in secular, culturally incredibly complex modes of experience, and yet as still referencing the mind of God to a quest for rational affiliation to experience as grounded in our own historically verified moment of meaning—Jesus (Taylor 2007; Smith 2014; McGrath 2000; Polkinghorne 2005; Craig 2008). Finally, the historical Jesus scholars, E. P. Sanders, John Dominic Crossan, N. T. Wright, and Geza Vermes, as examples, help us incorporate understanding into empirical disciplines, showing that Jesus' life can be seen as having actually happened and be brought forth as ethically captivating (Sanders 1993; Crossan 1991; Wright 1996; Vermes 1973).

For the contemporary reader, seeking the secular, scientific, or skeptical experience of meaning, Jesus emerges as the radical realist—traceable in history, transforming within ethics, and involved in relationality, as well as the authority of ultimate meaning. As a Christian, by providing a thoughtful integration of philosophy and theology traditions and historical scholarship, this Christology places Jesus within this relationality, indicating the Gospel continues to be genuinely relevant and to provide a multidimensional experience to have engagement with a figure whose life and teachings generate meaning and reason as illuminating of morality and the human condition.

Chapter One

RATIONALISM: JESUS AND THE LOGIC OF THE KINGDOM

ational thought places priority on reason, logic, and systematic order to the extent that they are the key ways we have of knowing anything. Since the Enlightenment, human cultures have relied on rational thought to organize aspects such as law, ethics, and scientific inquiry. In our life today, logic is frequently treated as the ultimate arbiter of truth—dictating everything from public policy decisions to our private morality. Rationalism is certainly a powerful way of knowing; however, rationalism has inherent limitations, all of which become apparent when we attempt to understand questions of ultimate meaning, moral dilemmas, or the depth of a relationship. To consider Jesus as

1

a rationalist reveals a unique dynamic. He engages human reason with precision, while simultaneously transcending it. He demonstrates that wisdom extends beyond formulaic thinking.

The Gospels demonstrate that Jesus consistently employed reason to teach, ask questions, and illuminate. The parable of the Good Samaritan (Luke 10:25–37) serves as a prime example. The question posed was "Who is my neighbor?" Jesus' response came in the form of a parable, which engaged the question of one's neighbor by exposing social and moral assumptions, thereby stimulating a response beyond conventional logic. Rational reasoning is certainly at play in this parable; yet the conclusion does not come by way of deduction or predictability, challenges social norms, and beckons ethical imagination. Similarly, when asked about paying taxes to Caesar (Matthew 22:15–22), Jesus employed a logically coherent approach, demonstrated moral reasoning, and navigated a politically charged dilemma with precision. Herein, the rationale used is relational, sensitive to context, and accountable to morality—an approach that foreshadows the ideas of Søren Kierkegaard, who maintained that an authentic encounter with Christ engages existential knowing, not abstract knowledge (Kierkegaard 1843, Fear and Trembling).

The fullness of the Kingdom of God cannot be contained solely within rationality. Paul informs the readers, "The wisdom of God is foolishness to men" (1 Corinthians 1:25), which informs that God's wisdom works supra-rationally. Jesus' teachings reflect a logic rooted in historical fact, ethical judgment, and relational nuance, yet cannot be simplified into a formula. Rationalism provides parameters from which patterns can be understood, decisions can be made, and outcomes predicted; rationalism also lacks resources for purpose, justice, or ultimate meaning. In this way, Jesus' reasoning also aligns with Thomas Aquinas, who promotes the interdependencies of reason and faith: human reason sees truth within natural philosophy, but ultimately, it is re-oriented toward God; (Aquinas 1274, Summa Theologica) to that end, rational thought is a means, and not an end unto itself and Jesus' displays logic that respects reason, but points beyond reason.

The narrative of the woman taken in adultery (John 8:1-11) is witness to this interdependence. Jesus employs reason to interrogate the crowd's moral assumptions: "He who is without sin among you, let him throw a stone first." The claim is constructed logically, which entreats self-reflection, while simultaneously being supra-rational in its injunction to mercy, accountability, and relational awareness. Reason is not abandoned; rather, it is refined and elevated, yielding insights that pure reason could never achieve. The relevant connections are re-sounded in Karl Barth's later description of Jesus as the living Word interrupting human presuppositions and displaying logic that cannot be separated from history and moral action (Barth 1936-1969, Church Dogmatics).In contemporary times, rationalism underpins almost all aspects of life. Data, algorithms, and evidence-based reasoning inform our decision-making, but ethical, relational, and existential questions often remain unaddressed. Jesus demonstrates that rationality alone is insufficient and requires ethical acumen and historical context. Jesus' reasoning is thoughtful, coherent, and orderly. Yet, it leads ultimately to the Kingdom, which is a reality beyond rationality. In this place, human reason comes together with divine wisdom, moral complexity, and relational truth. C.S. Lewis, with similar tools, once argued that reason and faith are complementary; it is only with faith's engagement with moral realities that reason itself is enhanced and oriented toward the good (Lewis 1952, Mere Christianity). When modern readers understand Jesus in this way, they can remain rational about the things of this world while also recognizing the psychological limitations of rationality alone.

Jesus' reasoning is also empirically grounded and could engage in constructive dialogue with contemporary perspectives about faith and science. Just as John Polkinghorne has said that empirical observations and relational insight can coexist (Polkinghorne 1989, Science and Providence), Jesus' reasoning was concerned with both observable reality and moral and relational implications. The story of feeding the 5,000 (Matthew 14:13–21) is a case in point—practical evaluation of hunger, resources, and sociological dynamics leads to a decision with immediate measurable effects, while also communicating ethical and spiritual realities. Rational evaluations are enriched through relational evaluations, revealing a pattern of decision-making that collectively attends to observation, discernment, and principled morality.

Even contemporary philosophers of religion are calling attention to the importance of reasoning within a relational and moral framework, aligned with the ones pursued by Craig and McGrath. Craig emphasizes that rational argumentation bolsters faith but does not replace the necessity of real engagement in relational and moral matters (Craig 2008, Reasonable Faith). McGrath suggests that science and theology engage complementary dimensions of human understanding (McGrath 2010, The Big Question). Jesus is the embodiment of this integration: logic and reason are actively and meaningfully engaged within the bounds of ethical discernment to the realities of history and relational knowledge.

Ultimately, rationalism, as modeled in the life of Jesus, is simultaneously rigorous and transcendent—engaging reason fully, observing reality accurately, and applying coherent logic, all the while leading to and then pointing to a reality that indeed exceeds rational logic—the Kingdom of God. Rational thought is always necessary, but never sufficient. Readers of Scripture are invited to learn that reason must also be engaged through a moral, relational, and historical context, while being shaped by principles that attend to human and divine moments. In sum, the logic of Jesus is not only directive but also transformative in how to live with uncertainty, complexity, and ethical dilemmas in coherent and principled ways.

The Meaning of Rationalism

Both the history and philosophy of rationalism emphasize the significant weight placed on reason—encompassing both deduction and logic-based reasoning—as the primary vehicle for knowing. In contrast to realism, which seeks truth in the observable, lived experience, and idealism, which privileges pure ideas, rationalism values order, coherence, and reasoned thought. It is interested in clarity and predictability, providing a schema for addressing both the natural and social worlds. Rationalist systems aim to create structures that explain phenomena, predict outcomes, and organize knowledge into derived hierarchies to achieve stability in an otherwise uncertain world. Historically, rationalism provided the foundations for modern debates on law, the scientific method, Enlightenment philosophy, and the technological and industrial revolutions. Its influence extends into modern social, political, and technological systems, resulting in a world in which governance, financial planning, education, health policy, and museum operations are all informed by algorithms, data analysis, and reasoning systems that proliferate decision-making processes. In many ways, rationalism reflects humanity's efforts to grapple with and understand the reality of being alive, aiming to achieve clarity, evidence, and disciplined intellectual rigor.

Rationalism demands that truth be coherent, logically sound, and subject to some systematic reasoning. Since the Enlightenment, rationalist thought has sustained itself as the normative framework for science, law, and modern education, emphasizing deduction, analytical reasoning, and logical inference. Rationalism encourages one to expect the universe to be understood by reason alone and that patterns of causality, predictability, and law can be identified and codified. Rationalism has inherent limitations; while it excels at guiding human understanding through the analysis of predictable systems, uncovering theories of underlying principles, and providing intellectual clarity, it also has its limitations. Rational methods for knowledge are far less helpful in answering moral, purposeful, or ultimate questions—they cannot fully illuminate why life matters, or how one should pursue justice in a complex social world, or what it means to live a life oriented toward higher ethical ideals. Rational analysis can help guide decision-making to a conclusion. Still, it cannot substitute for the need for ethical discernment, relational empathy in decision-making, or existential reflection.

In this sense, the life and teaching of Jesus represent a striking alternative to reason. Jesus coherently engages rationality in a relationship while moving beyond systematic logic. The parables He uses, the dialogues He engages in, and even the modes of moral provocations He employs to challenge the religious leaders make intellectual sense and, at the same time, invite reflective observations, ethical insights, and relational attention that do not occur when only using systems of rational calculation. Jesus models that rationality is necessary, but not enough; the Kingdom of God is supra-rational, a space where logic meets human history, lived experience, and moral discernment to create depth and relational insight. Jesus' teaching assumes that rationality must always be informed by wisdom, governed by ethical obligation, and informed

6

by non-quantifiable and non-systemizable relational realities. In this sense, Jesus offers an alternative perspective on how rational thinking, moral judgment, and relational action can come together to reveal a more holistic picture of truth, goodness, and human flourishing—ways that rationalism is limited to capture.

Jesus' Use of Reason

Jesus regularly utilizes reasoning through parables, questions, and dialogues. More than abstract teachings that hover above life's realities, Jesus' stories are meticulously constructed to lead people into reasoning, question previously held assumptions, and rouse them to reflect. Parables are not merely illustrative; they are invitations to use critical theorizing. The audience is engaged to think critically, propose meaning, and confront conflicts between expected logic and lived experiences. This engagement reflects Kierkegaard's insistence that the call to existential engagement with Christ requires concrete encounter rather than abstract engagement and speculation (Kierkegaard 1843, Fear and Trembling).

Let's consider an example of the effectiveness of a parable. In the parable of the Good Samaritan (Luke 10:25–37), the lawyer questions Jesus, "Who is my neighbor?" anticipating Jesus would give him a narrow and socially convenient answer. Instead, Jesus tells the story of a Samaritan (an outsider) who proves himself to be a good neighbor in his deeds of love towards a man in desperate need. Jesus creatively flips cultural expectations: the one fulfilling the law of love is not the priest and the Levite, both socially approved figures. The point is that Jesus forces the audience to rethink the societal logic of their norms. Still, he also deepens the inquiry beyond social identity, because whether someone is good or not cannot be simply determined by social value or religious identity. In this way, Jesus illustrates what C.S. Lewis would later articulate as the harmony of reason and moral imagination. All reasoning is fully exercised, but all reasoning is also constructed around ethical truth and relational reality (Lewis 1952, Mere Christianity). Jesus demonstrates, through engaging rationalism, that reasoning and logic can be seen as valid tools (and indeed are). Still, they are never sufficient, when standing alone, to be meaningful. He honors rational thinking and inquiry yet always points beyond rational inquiry into relational, ethical, and spiritual truths and realities. It is honored as a form of discerning right action, navigating moral paradoxes, and addressing relational complexities in human environments. But it will never be devoid of or separated from the ethical and spiritual dimensions of life that pure rationalism seems to fail to consider. Paul Tillich argues that true wisdom combines existential depth and rational clarity, asking both the "how" and the "why" in human action (Tillich 1951, Systematic Theology).

Even in the discussions with the Pharisees and Sadducees, Jesus uses questions to expose inconsistencies and contradictions in their reasoning. Jesus invites and engages the Pharisees and Sadducees to critically examine their thinking, weighing the evidence and principles at stake. This is an example of supra-rational logic: internally coherent, historically situated, and relationally contextual, yet not reducible to the boundaries of pure deductive logic. Rational thought is a productive path, not a robust destination--the reality Jesus describes as part of the Kingdom of God is a reality that coheres to logic and reasoning, yet transcends it as well. Likewise, Karl Barth notes how reasoning engages with and is transformed by the living Word, pointing to a deeper truth of God interacting with rational inquiry (Barth 1936–1969, Church Dogmatics).

Ultimately, the way Jesus engages with reasoning poses a challenge to both modernity and antiquity: relatedness must be integrated with moral reasoning, accompanied by an awareness of engaging histories. It is a rational, coherent, yet incomplete rationalism that fails to account for higher levels of existence and goodness. N.T. Wright's historical comments on how Jesus' reasoning can never be understood outside of its own social, political, and moral context of first-century life are a historical reality and a logic that takes action, shifts, and engages in reality rather than a theoretical disengagement about reality (Wright 1996, Jesus and the Victory of God). When Jesus engages in reasoning, it is disciplined, rigorous, consequential, yet also directed toward a Kingdom ethic of goodness that transcends mere calculations.

Supra-Rational Wisdom

The wisdom of Jesus continually shows that reason, no matter how powerful, has its own boundaries. Paul notes, "Because the foolishness of God is wiser than men, and the weakness of God is stronger than men" (1 Corinthians 1:25). Rational thought can measure, calculate, and systematize. Still, it cannot capture the moral paradoxes, relational dilemmas, or spiritual reality of the ways of the Kingdom of God. Jesus engages the intellect—but not as its prisoner. This invites comparison to Thomas Aquinas' engagement with reason and faith, wherein human reason points to divine truth but never exhausts it (Aquinas 1274, Summa Theologica).

His teaching utilizes and provides coherence on multiple levels. The teaching of parables provides a coherent narrative; yet, that rational story also conveys moral imperatives, spiritual truths, and a historical dimension. In considering the parable of the Prodigal Son (Luke 15:11–32), we recognize a story that is coherently framed in the rational world as a story of inheritance, choice, and consequence. However, it also conveys forgiveness, the restoration of relationships, and divine love that transcends rationality. The logic of the story gives meaning, but the wisdom sits above that which reason fully captures and structures. Kierkegaard discusses this layered engagement, suggesting the encounter with Christ requires an existential engagement that goes beyond abstract or formulaic engagements (Kierkegaard 1843, Fear and Trembling).

Supra-rational wisdom engages relational ethics. Jesus invites his audience to think critically, but then reminds the moral and relational impact of those decisions. Rationalism can shed light on behaviors, but it often lacks the capacity to see justice, mercy, or nuance in human relationships. Jesus' logic seamlessly draws these together. To understand the world, we employ ethical insight, historical context, and relational cognition. Paul Tillich observes that the ultimate truth binds the intellect and existential experience, or, to put it differently, reason and lived experience (Tillich 1951, Systematic Theology).

At the same time, the Kingdom of God is grounded in history, yet it captures something beyond the immediate. Rational analysis can measure causes and effects, identify patterns, and test hypotheses, but the teachings of Jesus remind us that the ultimate reality encompasses spiritual truth, eternal consequences, and divine purpose. As mentioned before, supra-rational wisdom captures coherence and systematic intelligibility. Still, it does not reduce to a human system of logic. The reason is respected. The logical systems are used rigorously, but lead toward something more than logic itself could capture. Charles Taylor observes that modern secularism is reasoned but still struggles to capture the transcendent meaning; yet, Jesus' teaching models a specific way of reasoning that is historical, relational, and spiritual (Taylor 2007, A Secular Age).

In this sense, rationalism and supra-rationalism are not in opposition but rather complementary. Reason is the means to understanding, and supra-rational wisdom shines light on the ethical, relational, and spiritual dimensions that rationality cannot capture. Modern readers, shaped by the scientific, industrial, and technological revolutions, can see the coherence of Jesus' reasoned ethical process, while also encountering issues that Jesus' wisdom is beyond the typical frameworks readers are accustomed to. Readers see an invitation to engagement as both a mental and a heart-centered experience. As Alister McGrath discusses, faith and reason enrich each other, demonstrating that scientific, historical, and philosophical inquiry does not stand opposed to relational and spiritual engagement (McGrath 2015, Science & Religion).

Rationalism in Ethical Decision-Making

Throughout Jesus' ministry, he exemplified the reasoned deliberation of a rationalist applied to difficult ethical dilemmas, revealing the limits of logic in the absence of moral discernment. For example, when the scribes and Pharisees bring a woman caught in adultery before Jesus and demand strict adherence to the Law—execution by stoning as prescribed in Deuteronomy—he offers reasoning that challenges both the accusers and the letter of the law. "He who is without sin among you, let him throw a stone first," (John 8:7). Rational thought is deployed here—inviting reflection on oneself and the logical consistency of the accusers—but the reasoning is steeped in relational and moral insight. Again, we see the inseparable nature of reason and ethics. This interplay is the same insight that Kierkegaard contended required engagement with truth beyond a purely abstract rationalist model—where existential self-reflection and ethical proposition are folded into reasoned engagement (Kierkegaard 1843, Fear and Trembling).

Similarly, when discussing the appropriateness of paying taxes to Caesar in Matthew 22:15–22, the Pharisees set a trap for Jesus. His reasoned response reflects thoughtful consideration of civic duty, spiritual allegiance, and social expectation; "Render therefore to Caesar the things that are Caesar's, and to God the things that are God's" (Matthew 22:21). A simple rational analysis of the dilemma alone would not be able to resolve that question. It requires discernment to wrestle with the question's historical considerations, moral reasoning, and relational process. Barth advances that understanding human and divine law together requires a theology of moral and ethical coherence that is historically informed by factual intelligence (Barth 1936–1969, Church Dogmatics).

What we see in these encounters is that rationalism can be a tool, rather than an unresolvable problem. For ethical reasoning to be effective, it must acknowledge the complexity of human experience, the nuanced relationships between individuals, and the consequential implications of broader moral realities. Jesus does not desire to abandon reason—he seeks to elevate it—showing that rational thought works best when it is coupled with ethical sensitivity and a historical relationship to the antecedents of the tragic dilemma. Likewise, Paul Tillich would define understanding as the convergence of rationality, existential awareness of being, and morality, demonstrating that rationality can only foster understanding through a comprehensive awareness (Tillich 1951, Vol. 1, 45).

Jesus' example remains extremely applicable today, particularly in a world dominated by procedural logic, algorithms, and rule-based systems. These lessons are ever-so-relevant. Rational frameworks tend to facilitate logical and efficient decisions, yet they rarely cultivate the nuanced judgment associated with morality. Jesus provides us with a model in which reason, ethics, and relational intelligence coexist in the same deliberative space. The ethical dilemmas we meet constantly—whether in law, business, or indecision in our own lives—are best engaged through a supra-rational disposition involving the logic of rationality and an appreciation for justice (moral), compassion (relational), and proposed outcomes (understanding, proving the indubitable truths of the past). N.T. Wright notes that the combined historical and ethical awareness through Jesus illustrates that ethical clarity cannot be exercised without discussions couched in discerning human responsibility, showing that practical agency must recognize reason, relational engagements, and moral reality (Wright 1996, Jesus and the Victory of God).

Jesus demonstrated rationalism. It is not the rigidity of being rule-based, or purely calculative logic, but discernment in all matters of reason that respects both reason and moral reality. Rational thought is definitely required, but wise judgments require the rational understanding of a judicious application within the realms of human dignity, relational complexity, and ethical integrity. In Jesus, modern readers encounter a model of holistic, reasoned engagement—a reasoned engagement that can be both pragmatic (applied) and more than pragmatic (supra-rational), yet coherent with moral and ethical righteousness.

Rational Faith in the 21st Century

Rationalist paradigms predominantly govern the contemporary world. In areas such as technology, science, economics, and law, reason, evidence, and reliable outcomes prevail. Rationalism shapes how we comprehend the universe, make decisions, and establish truth. In the context of a rationalist paradigm, faith is often depicted as irrational, emotional, or outdated. The Gospels, however, offer a model that incorporates rational thought as a means of engaging without reducing the Kingdom of God to pure logic.

Faith in Jesus - rightly understood - is not irrational; it is supra-rational. Reason is honored and engaged in the Gospel narratives; parables, dialogues, and moral quandaries invite critical thought, but these acts point beyond deduction to insights into ethics, relationships, and spirituality. Consider the story of the Good Samaritan (Luke 10:25-37): the reasons are clear, the conclusion moral, and yet the implications for relationships and counterculturalism surpass measurement. Rationality is important, but not sufficient; supra-rational wisdom encompasses ethics, empathy, and historical consciousness. Søren Kierkegaard asserts that genuine engagement with moral truth requires a leap beyond abstraction, where ethical richness cannot be separated from existential commitment (Kierkegaard 1843, Fear and Trembling). Or consider Paul Tillich's observation that rational inquiry needs existential awareness to make sense of the depths of the human experience (Tillich 1951, Systematic Theology).

Perhaps for a contemporary readership, we are interested in this integration. The rationalist way of thinking desires coherence and systematic understanding. Jesus offers coherence, too, but in a way that transcends rationalist reductionism. Human life is not just an engagement with guaranteed algorithmic processes or reasoning. We are called to engage with ethical judgment, moral imagination, and an awareness of historical significance. Rational faith demonstrates that reason serves insight, not stifles it. The intellect serves the human task of negotiating reality, but meaning and responsibility transcend mere calculation. Charles Taylor observes that in modern secular frameworks, we can often miss sources of moral or spiritual significance; yet, a rational, informed faith can bring coherence to lived experience, and significance in no way diminishes intellectual rigor (Taylor 2007, A Secular Age).

The supra-rational model of faith, moreover, challenges the reductions of modernity. Data, evidence, and scientific models can reveal patterns and predict outcomes, but do not provide sufficiently responsive answers to ultimate questions of purpose, value, or flourishing for humanity. Rational faith can bridge and address this deficit by highlighting the engagement of rational thought while also calibrating to ethical and spiritual realities, resulting in a system of thought that is coherent yet expansive, disciplined yet transcendent. N.T. Wright underscores the historical and rational foundations of Jesus' life for later ethical and theological reflection, and in a modern, skeptical context evidenced an impact of the life of Jesus over consideration of the earthly and eternal (Wright 1996, Jesus and the Victory of God).

In the 21st Century, to live in society with priorities of logic and empirical validation, this faith model claims relevance in contemporary culture. The rationalist mind does not dismiss thought; instead, it redirects it for renewed clarity of discernment, ethical clarity, and relational clarity. The development of supra-rational coherence logically does not ignore evidence; instead, it builds on it to demonstrate that Jesus' teachings are intellectually defensible while ethically provocative. In this model, the Kingdom of God serves as a supra-rational system, providing a standard for coherence of purpose and demonstrating that reason and faith are not contradictory opposites, but rather pathways to truth, meaning, and ethical engagement.

Chapter Two

EMPIRICISM: WHAT WE CAN SEE VS. WHAT WE BELIEVE

The Meaning of Empiricism

*E*mpiricism, as both a philosophical and scientific epistemology, insists that knowledge is acquired through experience, observation, and evidence. Locke's assertion that all knowledge comes from the mind as a blank slate, then utters sensory or phenomenal experience, represents a caution or support for evidence-based study of reality (Locke, An Essay Concerning Human Understanding, 1690), as does Hume's insistence that human understanding itself is grounded in empirical impressions (Hume, An Enquiry Concerning Human Understanding, 1748). The scientific revolution - which included the telescopic discoveries of

Galileo, laws of motion discovered by Newton, and the laws of planetary motion discovered by Kepler - embodied the promise of empiricism: the world could be systematically observed, measured, and accurately predicted (Galileo, Dialogues Concerning Two New Sciences, 1638; Newton, Principia Mathematica, 1687).

However, while powerful and stunningly effective as a means of deciphering natural regularities and material processes, empirical reasoning and observation struggle with something more life-altering: meaning, purpose, and moral or ethical insight. How does the empirical method reckon with justice, mercy, or relate to the multidimensionality of human existence? It is into precisely this space that the life of Jesus demonstrates a unique complementarity. The ministry of Jesus engages with the observable and verifiable - the towns He visited, the identifiable individuals He healed, and the crucifixion and resurrection that were witnessed by those in the time period (Mark 2:1-12), while also pointing beyond the immediately measurable to ethical, spiritual, or relational truths. Jesus is a model of a way of empirical, observational, experiential engagement that quests for moral and existential significance, indicating that observation and experience are not an end in themselves. Empiricism is accessed through observable and experiential means, but it is a portal to something more profound.

Historically and philosophically, theologians and historians have wrestled with this dimension of faith and empiricism. Thomas Aquinas serves as an example of pre-modern synthesis: human reason and observation can illuminate natural law, to which we can ultimately aspire in our pursuit of divine reality. However, ethical and spiritual truths surpass sense data (Aquinas, Summa Theologica, 1265-1274). Blaise Pascal, in Pensées, acknowledges both the limits of rational calculation and the necessity of a personally lived experience of God, anticipating the friction between physical experience and existential experience in faith (Pascal, Pensées, 1670). In the modern period, Søren Kierkegaard argues that genuine knowledge of Christ is not merely abstract/rational, but rather existential, lived, and confrontational; however, this tenet complements empiricism by insisting on the fact of human experience as the site of knowing (Kierkegaard, Fear and Trembling, 1843).

In the contemporary context, theologians and philosopher-scientists continue the conversation. For example, Karl Barth recognizes Jesus as the Word, who existed in a contained history that cannot be reduced to measurable abstraction, thereby confronting human thought (Barth, Church Dogmatics, 1932-1969). Paul Tillich integrates existential philosophy and Christian theology, suggesting that the questions of meaning, anxiety, and purpose must be lived out in both reality and the transcendental (Tillich, Systematic Theology, 1951-1963). C. S. Lewis, in Mere Christianity and The Abolition of Man, demonstrates how empirical observation of human behavior can reveal moral truth, but moral reason must have a transcendent basis that extends beyond the measurable (Lewis, 1952; 1943).

For a scientifically literate public, thinkers like John Polkinghorne and Alister McGrath present reason and faith as not in opposition. Polkinghorne's identity as both a physicist and a theologian demonstrates that empirical observation, recognition of patterns, and inferring causation can exist with ethical and spiritual consideration (Polkinghorne, Science and Providence, 1989). McGrath also points out that scientific and theological inquiry can, and should, complement each other. He stresses that empirical and historical inquiries can enrich one's faith, rather than supplant it (McGrath, Science & Religion, 2011).

Engaging with empirical observation and evidence also aligns with contemporary secular perspectives. Charles Taylor discusses secularism and how it challenges us to find meaningfulness in a world governed by facts and measurable effects (Taylor, A Secular Age, 2007). William Lane Craig discusses the tension between evidence and metaphysical claims, showing that one can rationally examine observable reality without compromising conviction in one's acceptance of faith (Craig, Reasonable Faith, 2008). James K. A. Smith reminds us that cultural habits are formative to our encounters with both empirical and spiritual claims, and instead of denying either empirical notions or spiritual articulations, we should look for a nuanced alternative that engages the world through observability, formation, and praxis (Smith, How (Not) to Be Secular, 2014).

Scholars of the historical Jesus offer insight and clarification of the empirical roots of faith. E.P. Sanders and John Dominic Crossan provided an empirical study of Jesus' life and ministry. They established the significance of events that can be verified and tested, while also recognizing the interpretive addition of moral and spiritual significance (Sanders, The Historical Figure of Jesus, 1993; Crossan, The Historical Jesus, 1991). Together, Sanders and Crossan provide a bridge between the empirically observable and the morally or spiritually meaningful interpretations of those observable events. Together, they demonstrate the idea that faith and evidence complement each other, and are more informative and less optimal when 'decoupled.'

In this way, Jesus provides us with a model of empiricism that approximates our modern sensibilities through observable, historical acts of ministry such as healing the blind, feeding the hungry, and relating with social outcasts and the marginalized. Each of these acts or events is observable, historical, and verifiable—yet also holds considerable ethical, relational, or spiritual weight in consideration of the empirical act. The observation and its subsequent verification, which accompany empirical inquiry, only become meaningful when considered in conjunction with ethical considerations, relational awareness, and spiritual insights (Taylor, A Secular Age, 2007). Faith is not a denial of the facts; rather, it adds dimensions of moral and existential meaning and interpretation to those observable, historical events.

When contextualized within this dialogue—whether historical, theological, philosophical, or modern secular—empiricism becomes a site of engagement for readers to encounter human beings utilizing observations of demonstrable patterns and evidential meaning-making that aim to describe the human experience without reducing it to only what is objectively/measurably observable. In likeness, Jesus gives us a lived example of whole empiricism: as observers, testable, verifiable, etc., all the while affirming the ethical, relational, and spiritual paradigms with which he engaged, whilst being observable.

For modern readers, scientists, skeptics, and others, the idea of faith-in-action presents a challenge. Jesus, as a historical figure, enters the world, experience, and relationships in which human experience exists, affirming the power of experience while inviting interpretation or meaning-making beyond empirical exploration or sensory verification.

Jesus and the Empirical Lens

The event of Jesus with Thomas, "Doubting Thomas" (John 20:24-29), exemplifies vividly the tension between evidence-based knowledge and knowing through relationship, ethics, and spirituality. Thomas asks for evidence and declares that he must "see" the risen Jesus and "touch" him to believe. Thomas' requirement for evidence is consistent with the efforts toward empiricism presented by John Locke and David Hume, who reflected on knowledge that is derived from sensory experience and rejected anything that could not be verified (Locke, An Essay Concerning Human Understanding, 1690; Hume, An Inquiry Concerning Human Understanding, 1748). Thomas represents the rational preoccupation with certainty and demands that his faith conform to some observable evidence.

Jesus' sensible response to both the ancient and contemporary reader of scraps is the invitation to see and touch the wounds: "Reach your finger here, and look at My hands; and reach your hand here, and put it into My side. Do not be unbelieving, but believing." (John 20:27). To model for Thomas that empirical verification should not be in opposition to faith, even if empirical evidence is not at the forefront of the experience. Jesus accepts Thomas's level of evidence; instead, Jesus affirms observable evidence but moves Thomas beyond empirical evidence into the realm of relationship and ethics. Evidence serves as the bridge between rational verification and supra-rational experience.

At the same time, Jesus places limits on empiricism when he states, "Thomas, because you have seen Me, you have believed." "Blessed are those who have not seen and have believed" (John 20:29). Observation alone cannot capture the complete ethical, relational, and spiritual dimensions of an event. Blaise Pascal's reflections on existence in Pensées echo this idea when he asserts that human thought and empirically grounded calculations cannot fully account for the experience of faith and encounter with God (Pascal, 1670). Similarly, Søren Kierkegaard asserts that the existential encounter with Christ is an experience that transcends rational and sensory understanding; knowing God occurs through lived experiences, not mere observation (Kierkegaard, Fear and Trembling, 1843).

The modern theological conversation often brings philosophers and scientists into the dialogue. For example, Karl Barth highlights "Jesus as the historically real Word, which stands – one way or another – against the thought of men," and insists that autonomy of thought does not remove human thought from a real engagement with reality and a relational, ethical understanding (Barth, Church Dogmatics, 1932–1969). John Polkinghorne demonstrates that a scientifically literate position, which uses observation and causality to interpret reality, is perfectly compatible with ethical and spiritual reflection (Polkinghorne, Science and Providence, 1989). Similarly, E.P. Sanders and John Dominic Crossan, who explore the historical veracity of Jesus' actions, have offered empirical validation about Jesus that does not reduce actions solely to measurable phenomena (Sanders, The Historical Figure of Jesus, 1993; Crossan, The Historical Jesus, 1991). These conversations provide further evidence that models where evidence and faith inform each other are an accepted hermeneutic and epistemology of faith.

In a contemporary context, Thomas' story resonates with a society constantly inundated with data, analytics, and empirical metrics. Skepticism is increasingly justified, and society continually searching for proof before engaging in moral or spiritual practices is a common occurrence. Jesus illustrates a rational, yet balanced approach: evidence serves as a marker to engage and even validate, but it is not the sole arbiter of truth. Jesus honored the rational verification of the disciples and Thomas, all the while glutting it with ethical reflection, historical awareness, and relational trust. William Lane Craig offers a similar perspective, suggesting that the coexistence of reason and evidence with morality and existential reasoning produces a coherent framework for belief in an increasingly literate and rational society (Craig, Reasonable Faith, 2008). James K.A. Smith also underscores the role of habits, cultural formation, and reflective engagement in human interpretation of evidence and subsequent action (Smith, How (Not) to Be Secular, 2014).

Thomas offers a model for empirical engagement that neither dismisses observation nor elevates observation as sufficient. Jesus clearly argues that sense evidence affords access to deeper ethical, relational, and spiritual realities. In this, Thomas's encounter teaches the modern reader attempting to navigate an increasingly measurable world that faith is informed by reason and observation, yet transcends reason. Faith allows a modern reader to embrace the empirical, yet not remain confined to it. Therefore, the story provides a starting point for a better understanding of how experience relates to historical details and evidence, as well as the intersection of trust and lived experience —a clear example and template for engaging with this empirical challenge in the 21st century.

Faith Beyond Sight (Supra-Empiricism)

Thomas's interaction with the risen Christ illustrates the significance and limitation of empirical verification. Confronted with sensory verification, Jesus turned toward a deeper engagement in faith that is not limited by empirical verification (John 20:24–29). This kind of "supra-empirical" faith demonstrates that human sense, and the evidence witnesses observe, despite necessity, cannot solely convey the moral, relational, and spiritual meanings that are communicated in Christ.

The resurrection itself serves as a historical anchor for this claim. Unlike allegorical and mythical constructs, the Gospels document the resurrection as an event in a particular time and place with multiple witnesses (Luke 24:1–12; 1 Corinthians 15:3–8). The historical event addresses some of E.P. Sanders' and John Dominic Crossan's concerns about how to understand Jesus.' Others, such as Sanders and Crossan, have elaborated on his human, first-century historical context (Sanders, The Historical Figure of Jesus, 1993; Crossan, The Historical Jesus, 1991). However, the actual meaning of the resurrection, as it relates to forgiveness, reconciliation, and restoration, is not limited to how humans can empirically observe. Therefore, the resurrection also invites a supra-rational, interpretive engagement with the event. Blaise Pascal captures these sentiments regarding the necessity of human evaluation of God while arguing that experience often requires a leap of insight to engage both our heart and our intellect (Pascal, Pensées, 1670).

Supra-empiricism also acknowledges the difference between empirical reality and socio-moral and relational realities. Thomas observes and concedes that his wounds are indeed physical. However, the ethical and spiritual meanings—the reconciliation, the call to discipleship, the inaugurated Kingdom—cannot be evaluated. Søren Kierkegaard's existential emphasis on the immediacy of individual experience with Christ illustrates this point: human knowledge of God must be personal, lived, and relational, rather than being reduced to data or formulaic reasoning (Kierkegaard, Fear and Trembling, 1843). Karl Barth also places Jesus as the historically real and morally active Word, which cannot be fully known to sight alone (Barth, Church Dogmatics, 1932-1969).

For modern readers navigating a data-centric culture, there are profound lessons to be learned from this model. While technology, metrics, quantifiables, infrastructure, and measurable outcomes are ever-present in today's decision-making, empirically based evidence of the experience of phenomenological meaning offers little guidance in determining purpose, virtue, or relational flourishing. Jesus' encounter with Thomas serves as a balance in epistemology: observable evidence is confirmed, yet knowledge of the truth reaches beyond sense experience. John Polkinghorne's analysis in Science and Providence exemplifies how a scientifically literate worldview could afford space for ethical and spiritual meaning, a position characterized as logically coherent, in which observation and interpretation are mutually co-efficient categories of interpretation (Polkinghorne, 1989).

Lane Craig and James K.A. Smith have also discussed the intersection of empirical evidence and supra-empirical faith. Craig clarifies that, both historically and normatively, evidence is used to provide a rational foundation for faith; however, we must also take into account moral and existential reflection when pursuing Christian truth (Craig, Reasonable Faith, 2008). On the other hand, Smith proposes that cultural and interpretive habits shape the process of attempting to make sense of the evidence, which means we need a reflective perspective that transcends the limitations of a purely empirical view (Smith, How (Not) to be Secular, 2014). In this sense, supra-empirical faith can also be understood as interactive in the mediational space: it operates, to some extent, concerning observation and knowledge, "measures" the moral, relational, and spiritual consequences of human flourishing beyond empirical evidence.

The lesson is straightforward: faith does not ask us to abandon reason or the evidence, nor must it be contained by them. Supra-empirical meaning in all requires discernment, reflection, and consciousness of history. The story of Thomas' faith is both grounded and transcendent; substantively in observable reality, and sanctified by the moral and ethical spirit of evidence-informed reality. For contemporary readers, this model provides practical pathways for navigating a world filled with metrics and measurable outcomes, while maintaining a focus on relational engagement, ethical insight, and spiritual discernment. This framework encompasses empiricism, as well as the fuller richness of reality, including human, ethical, and divine dimensions, which can be experienced again when observable reality is present once more.

Historical Grounding: Evidence and Testimony

Empiricism underscores that such knowledge is determined through observation, measurement, and verification. In terms of Jesus' life and the early Christian movement, this is a significant point: faith is not just ethereal speculation or myth, but is based on history and eyewitness testimony. The resurrection, at the center of the Christian claim, is an event recorded in several independent accounts that enjoy remarkable consensus (Luke 24:1–12; 1 Corinthians 15:3–8). Paul notes a historical verifiability, stating that the risen Christ appeared to "more than five hundred brethren at once, of whom the greater part remain to the present, but some have fallen asleep" (1 Corinthians 15:6). As an example of empiricism, these are claims that are obtainable from reality and not just imagination alone.

The historical basis of faith is also in line with the research of E.P. Sanders and N.T. Wright, who argues that understanding Jesus requires placing him within first-century Judean society (Sanders, The Historical Figure of Jesus, 1993; Wright, Jesus and the Victory of God, 1996). Both authors note that the Gospel writers consistently placed the events of Jesus' life within verifiable political, social, and geographic contexts: Roman occupation under Pontius Pilate as governor, conflicts with the temple authorities, and various social hierarchies in Galilee (Luke 3:1–2). Such verifications offer independent reference points that can also be understood under empiricist principles of measurement and plausibility. However, these same settings and varying contexts indicate something beyond the details of facts - namely, the ethical, relational, and spiritual implications thereof, or what can be understood as a supra-empirical dimension that reason and observation alone cannot provide.

The interplay between empirical reference points and their broader supra-empirical significance can be philosophically evaluated in the light of Blaise Pascal's insistence that faith applies both the mind and the heart (Pensées, 1670). Rational inquiry may validate the historical claims, while reflecting on the relational and ethical meanings of the claims provides interpretation. Similarly, Søren Kierkegaard emphasizes that one's encounter with Christ is rooted existentially and immediately, which entails applying one's personal response to the historical engagement rather than abstract speculation (Fear and Trembling, 1843). Despite its historical significance, Karl Barth asserts that Jesus—as a historical and morally active Word—can and ought to refer to things beyond empirical observation (Church Dogmatics, 1932–1969).

To speak of the historical basis and to invite critical engagement. Academic authors, such as John Dominic Crossan (The Historical Jesus, 1991), outline that if there is any value to be gained from investigating miracles, moral teachings, or the resurrection, it is best done within the cultural and temporal context. Rational, empirically recognized evaluation does not have to be anti-faith. It can facilitate trust that reflects both rationality and faith, exemplifying that evidence and belief are not mutually exclusive. Alister McGrath engages in the integration of forms through the juxtaposition of scientific reasoning with theological reflection, illustrating the points of mutual confirmation between historical inquiry and spiritual awakening (McGrath, Science & Religion, 2009).

For present-day readers in an empirically data-driven culture, this tension is shown to hold credibility and coherence with their understanding of emergent reality. Historical evidence provides an outlet that legitimizes belief. While the engagement with the moral and relational nature of the event is equally assuring, it also ensures that the significance to the faith remains spiritually enriched. Ultimately, in this arena, empiricism and supra-empirical significance are presented not as contradictory entities, but rather complementary lenses through which a person can encounter observable reality while also responding from ethical or existential spaces.

Faith and Modern Empirical Challenges

In the twenty-first century, empirical reasoning has a profound impact on nearly every aspect of human life. Science, technology, and practical evidence dictate how society evaluates claims, understands phenomena, and makes decisions. Whether for public policy or personal choices, there is an implicit premise that knowledge must be seen, measured, and replicated. Thus, religious faith tends to be treated sceptically in this cultural milieu: if faith cannot be seen, examined, or measured, is it valid or meaningful?

The story of Thomas, who is confronted with the resurrection claims of his colleagues, provides a more challenging context for addressing this skepticism (John 20:24–29). Thomas insists on empirical evidence, stating that he will not believe until he "sees in his hands the print of the nails" and "puts his finger into the print of the nails" (John 20:25). The resurrected Jesus appears to Thomas. He welcomes this empirical inquiry without judgment or condemnation. He invites Thomas to verify the physical reality of the resurrected body. Yet at the same time, Jesus offers this declaration: "Blessed are those who have not seen and yet have believed" (John 20:29). Jesus presents a dual epistemological position that values empirical verification but acknowledges that faith extends beyond the limitations of the senses.

The engagement of Thomas parallels, both philosophically and historically, the perspective reflected by Blaise Pascal, particularly in his writings about the interplay between reason and faith, where empirical and existential dimensions converge to create understanding (Pensées, 1670). Also, Søren Kierkegaard emphasizes the immediacy of the existential encounter with Christ, maintaining that knowing and understanding arise through a relationship with the historical reality and personal encounter, rather than abstraction or empiricism (Fear and Trembling, 1843). Thomas' epistemic approach resonates with readers who negotiate meaning in a culture that emphasizes data, observation, and reproducibility.

Modern thinkers continue this engagement. N.T. Wright and E. P. Sanders claim that the resurrection and the life of Jesus are historical events that can be studied critically as humans while retaining religious significance (Wright, Jesus and the Victory of God, 1996; Sanders, The Historical Figure of Jesus, 1993). In addition, Alister McGrath presents the observation that scientific literacy does not negate belief. That inquiry and theological reflection can inform one another (McGrath, Science & Religion, 2009). Finally, John Polkinghorne, writing from physics and theological perspectives, recognizes that evidence and insight coexist between evidence of reason and spiritual reasoning, and develops an approach to the rational examination of faith (Polkinghorne, Science and Providence, 1989).

In practical terms, the modern empirical orientation can be seen in Thomas's skepticism: individuals will not entertain extraordinary thoughts without observable proof. The account of Christianity in the Gospels takes skepticism into account but does not reduce the faith experience to empirical evidence. Belief in Jesus can be approached historically, through narrative, and through relational evidence. Yet, it goes into realms that cannot be quantified. There is an empirical dimension that guides understanding. Still, there is also a supra-empirical and transcendent reflection to give wisdom and meaning.

But in twenty-first-century terms, the lesson learned is straightforward: the empirical mindset does not obviate moral, ethical, or spiritual meaning and depth. When faith is grounded in history and observation, it can be examined with reasoned skepticism. Yet, it can also encompass dimensions of reality that defy measurement. Thus, an inquiry into Jesus' teachings could lead modern believers to practice a reflective, responsible, and discerning faith that honors the evidence while also understanding the ethical, relational, and transcendent nature of life.

Living Between Evidence and Trust

Contemporary existence often feels suspended between what can be established and what can be trusted. Empiricism provides greater servitude to the exploration of the material world through its use of observations, measurements, and repeated experience. At the same time, it fails to reach into meaning, purpose, and responsibility. The life of Jesus, according to the Gospels, gives us a model for balancing "evidence" with trust in matters that our five senses do not fully verify.

Thomas' encounter with the risen Christ (John 20:24-29) serves as a thought-provoking case in point. Jesus affirms Thomas' request for empirical "proof," while at the same time, expresses that those who believe, yet have not seen, are blessed. This dual tension creates a disciplined balance: reason and evidence inform understanding, while trust allows for a deeper capacity for relational, moral, and spiritual apprehension. One can recognize the limitations of what their senses provide while fully engaging in the deeper meaning of what is happening around them.

Philosophers and theologians also seem to appreciate this tension. For instance, Blaise Pascal speaks, in Pensées (1670), of the heart as a form of knowing that differs from reason. Søren Kierkegaard aspires to an existential encounter with Jesus that is more than an intellectual experience (Fear and Trembling, 1843). N.T. Wright and E.P. Sanders take Jesus out of the realm of theology and place him in history. Faith is grounded in real, historical events, as opposed to being reduced to abstractions (Wright, Jesus and the Victory of God, 1996; Sanders, The Historical Figure of Jesus, 1993). Similarly, John Polkinghorne and Alister McGrath argue that scientific literacy and empirical reasoning need not be in opposition to faith; evidence and trust can coexist as part of a coherent epistemology (Polkinghorne, Science and Providence, 1989; McGrath, Science & Religion, 2009).

For present-day readers, "evidence-informed trust" carries practical significance. In scientific or technical settings, we rely on data, models, and experiments to inform our decisions and determine a path forward. In personal and ethical living, many decisions are made within a context of uncertainty, weighing the probabilities, risks, and relational dimensions. The Gospel approach attempts to bring these two forms of knowing into relationship: observing and rational analysis do not negate faith, nor does faith require abandoning our reasoning faculties. Trust is an informed order of being, an engagement with realities that are both real and a reality that fits into a framework that is more than we can empirically account for.

This mode of being offers a pertinent counterpoint to the widespread skepticism prevalent today in a scientifically rational and empirically inclined society. Even individuals who are informed or interested in evidence can critique religious or ethical claims as "unverified" or "unfounded" as a result of being shaped or molded by epistemologies that prioritize data. The Gospels serve as an example. They remind us to proceed through life by rigorously observing what we can observe and rationally considering what we can know is true, even if it is not observable in a sensory way. Following the model of Jesus, we are practicing an order of thinking that respects the observable, while respecting and being open to the supra-sensory.

For practical implications in everyday life, relationships, community life, ethical decisions, and reflecting on the past all require a judgment that is beyond what we can say or quantify for the observed. Belief and trust in these spheres are not irrational, illogical, or incomprehensible exercises; there is historical, contextual, and relational evidence that contributes to our belief or trust. In relation to the Gospel model, contemporary readers may learn to live with uncertainty, responsibly interpret the evidence observed in daily life, and form trust in the unobserved, doing so within the same interplay of thinking that Jesus did.

Living within evidence and trust is not a compromise or a half-measure; it is an integrated order of discipline. It allows present-day people to engage consciously and rigorously with the world, while remaining open to a deeper understanding of what is true, moving about with a sense of the connection between empirical investigation and knowledge of ethical, relational, and spiritual truths- a connection or balance we cannot gain exclusively through empirical investigation.

Empiricism and the Historical Jesus

In its classical definition, empiricism posits that knowledge comes fundamentally from our senses—what we can see, hear, touch, and measure. This epistemological model has been at the heart of modern scientific thought; its ripple effect can be seen in the ways we approach history, philosophy, and the social sciences today (Locke, An Essay Concerning Human Understanding, 1690; Hume, An Inquiry Concerning Human Understanding, 1748). To apply an empirical gaze to the life of Jesus is both a tension and a truth. The Gospels recount stories that exceed the limits of regular sensory verification. Still, they are also deeply rooted in historical time and space, making them viable historical topics for examination and analysis.

The Gospels give us specific historical markers: the reign of Tiberius Caesar, the governorship of Pontius Pilate, and the high priesthood of Caiaphas (Luke 3:1–2). These markers ground the accounts in real, experienced circumstances for inquiry. Archaeological findings, historical records, and comparative studies of first-century Judea offer evidence of the world Jesus inhabited, where he moved, interacted, and taught. While we cannot use the kinds of empirical practices in social science or the sense of modern scientific verification in the investigation of miracles, we can use empirical practices to remit the cultural, political, and social trends present in the text, to understand the plausibility and context of Jesus' ministry (Wright, Jesus and the Victory of God, 1996; Sanders, The Historical Figure of Jesus, 1993).

Thomas, the disciple with doubts, epitomizes the tension between empirical realities and faith (John 20:24-29). Thomas's demand for sensory proof of the resurrected Jesus recalls a natural human tendency to want to believe based on evidence. Jesus is willing to entertain this rational method of verification, inviting Thomas to "touch the wounds," but elevates the idea of faith: "Blessed are those who have not seen and yet have believed" (John 20:29). While empirical evaluation is given space and dignity, it is not the only vehicle for discovering knowledge. The historic figure of Jesus invites us to simultaneously consider what is observable and what lies beyond observation, with a fusion of empirical observation and relational, ethical, and spiritual awareness (Kierkegaard, Fear and Trembling, 1843; Pascal, Pensées, 1670).

Empirical thinking in the gospels intersects at many points with forms of reasoning that already exist in legal and historical rationale. Eyewitness testimony, repetitions, and communal memory serve as forms of evidence already recognized as valid in scholarly and judicial contexts. In 1 Corinthians 15, Paul plainly articulates the notion that the resurrection was witnessed by numerous people, many of whom were still alive at the time of Paul's writing. This again encapsulates a sense of multiple-source evidence, which embodies proto-empirical rationality. Our acceptance of belief is based on grounded historical claims, with an acknowledgment that there is a level of acceptance that cannot be obtained by empirical measures (Polkinghorne, Science and Providence, 1989; McGrath, Science & Religion, 2009).

From this perspective, the historical Jesus is neither a myth nor an idea only, but a historical figure real to the lived experiences of that time period, accessible for investigation and analysis, providing truths about which one cannot sustain sensory verification. Empirical modes of thinking enable the understanding of method; another way of thinking about evidence only resolves the value of historicity by epistemological limitations (historicism). For example, one can use an epistemology of historicism, or evidence and data, to explain context, plausibility, and culture; however, it does not extend beyond the empirical to the supra-empirical. Modern readers who live in a world saturated with data, evidence, observable phenomena, etc. experience tension between what would be the realities of the times of Jesus, but also the relational, ethical, and meaning making truths revealed in Jesus' ministry; methods simultaneously claim both historical reality, and experiential and historically plausibility too (Lewis, Mere Christianity, 1952; Taylor, A Secular Age, 2007).

Balancing Faith and Evidence Today

In the 21st century, the role of empiricism is prevalent not only in science but also in public discourse, education, and personal decision-making. Increasingly, individuals seek evidence of the claims presented to them, measurable outcomes, and observable realities before they postulate truth. In light of this reality, the person and teachings of Jesus offer a way to reconcile awareness of empirical realities with concurrent trust in something transcendent. The Gospels do not posit a rejection of reality or reason; instead, they reveal a way of being in which empirical experience and historical consciousness can coexist with ethical, moral, and spiritual knowledge (Locke, An Essay Concerning Human Understanding, 1690; Hume, An Inquiry Concerning Human Understanding, 1748).

Thomas's story is illustrative. His request to see and touch Jesus is a natural impulse, given the context of his prior assumptions about sense verification and credibility (John 20:24–29). Jesus' response is illuminating. He provides Thomas with adequate observation to recognize the truth. Jesus then frames the significance of faith: trust beyond the immediate verification of sense experience. This brief exchange affirms a nuanced awareness of empiricism—evidence can inform, guide, and strengthen belief, while also acknowledging that some truths transcend empirical verification (Kierkegaard, Fear and Trembling, 1843; Pascal, Pensées, 1670). Modern scholarship may reveal a layered epistemology; data and observation will inform understanding, but this understanding must also be balanced with moral reasoning, historical reflection, and relational discernment (Polkinghorne, Science and Providence, 1989; McGrath, Science & Religion, 2009).

Moreover, historical documentation provides evidence for this integration. The Gospels are situated within specific, historical events, places, and encounters. Furthermore, Luke states that he conducted a careful investigation of the witnesses (Luke 1:1–4). Paul references multiple witnesses of the resurrection (1 Corinthians 15:3–8). These textual exercises effectively suggest that the early church was committed to verifiable history. Faith in Jesus, then, is not blind acceptance. Faith engages with evidence and ethical-moral interpretation (Wright, Jesus and the Victory of God, 1996; Sanders, The Historical Figure of Jesus, 1993).

What we draw from this is the possibility of developing a rational faith that honors empirical reality while also embracing supra-empirical realities. In personal and communal ethics (e.g., social justice) both believers and non-believers are challenged to negotiate evidence and values. Charitable action, perhaps, is corroborated by observable outcomes (i.e., reducing hunger, improving education). Yet, much of charitable action or community justice operates with an ethical and moral commitment, as well as relational empathy, that cannot be investigated or measured. Likewise, Jesus' teaching on mercy, forgiveness, and community necessitate a participation that goes beyond evidence, stating, or proving, beyond purely statistical or sensory experiences (Lewis, Mere Christianity, 1952; Taylor, A Secular Age, 2007).

Consequently, empiricism, when viewed from the perspective of Jesus' teaching, is neither a barrier to faith, but rather a facilitating factor in a faith story rooted in empirical experience. Faith can facilitate scrutiny, reflection, and analytical thinking, while still leaving room for a principle or reality that exists beyond immediate empirical observation. This rational engagement could provide a meaningful framework for living into the relevance (or meaning) of Jesus' teachings in a 21st-century disciple. In a world of data, experimentation, and measurable proof, faith and evidence are not mutually exclusive; they are two epistemologies that challenge us to take ethical action, foster relational awareness, and gain historical understanding in our human endeavors.

Chapter Three

PRAGMATISM: DOES FOLLOWING JESUS "WORK?"

The Meaning of Pragmatism

Pragmatism asserts that truth is based on outcomes and asks if beliefs, actions, or principles "work" to achieve meaningful consequences. When we connect Jesus to a pragmatist approach, we see an intriguing combination of immediate usefulness and lasting relevance. To be sure, Jesus' ministry produced observable benefits: He healed the sick, fed the hungry, taught crowds in various contexts, and restored communities. These actions produced palpable effects on individuals and communities, evidence of practical wisdom consistent with a pragmatist perspective (James 1907; Dewey 1938). From an outcome-based approach, Jesus was very effective in alleviating suffering and demonstrating ethical care.

However, He also wrong-footed traditional levels of practicality. His calls to self-denial, sacrificial love, and costly discipleship appear impractical from every worldly perspective (Matthew 16:24–26). Pragmatism, if the definition used is narrow, might characterize these teachings, or teachings like them, as ineffective or irrational. However, within the biblical framework of utility, the measure of practical utility extends beyond immediate material benefits. Practical utility necessitates evaluating relational transformation, moral concern, ethical growth, and flourishing in the spiritual, familial, and broader communal sense (Peirce 1878; Wright 2006). Pragmatism is just the beginning, then, but moral imagination, historical awareness, and supra-practical insight will open up the most whole dimension of understanding his impact.

Let's consider, as an illustration, the account of Jesus feeding the five thousand (John 6:1–14). What is beyond reproach is that a "pragmatic" outcome of that event was the immediate experience of relief from hunger (an observable outcome). It also pointed to more profound truths about human dependence on God, compassion for others, and the spiritual experience of Christ's provision. Like all the events in Jesus' life, the story employs pragmatism to limit our understanding of experience and meaning. The insight extends far beyond observable benefits alone, as seen in the example of feeding the five thousand, which is akin to saying the same thing while diffusing the illustration. Jesus' ethical teachings, such as turning the other cheek, loving your enemies, and forgiving debts, also have the capacity to impact deeper relationships, resulting in long-term practical outcomes that do not simply register or measure by the expected cultural and practical terms of success and remedy (James 1907; Tillich 1951).

Of course, modern readers are more than capable of engaging in a pragmatic lens in a culture of accountable outcomes, efficiency, measurable progress, and a drive toward discovering proof of every other type. However, the life of Jesus reveals that any suggestion of "work," of following Him, cannot be reduced to efficiency, expediency, or observable effectiveness. Faith, discipleship, and moral development are efficient approaches or practices, as they develop character, relational integrity, and a teleological view of humans flourishing both historically and contextually (Dewey 1938; James 1907). Engaging Jesus pragmatically requires discerning and weighing both immediate relative consequences and sustained "depth," in the form of dimensions of significance, ethical integrity, and relational connectedness.

One implication of acting pragmatically is that pragmatism and the concept of accountability are not the only tools for estimating usefulness, but they can be applied as a process of evaluation. Practical outcomes evaluate a notion of usable benefit, yet overarching this is the assessment of accurate outcomes that call us to sustainable change, virtue, and evidence of flourishing in relational, moral, and spiritual ways. Jesus' life invites us to a broader pragmatism. It illustrates practical ethical action that has no distinction between good ethical vision, historical affect, and sustainability in relation to God and others.

Jesus' Practical Ministry

Jesus' ministry demonstrates a purposeful engagement with pragmatic instances, illustrating components of the pragmatic principle, whereby we should pursue truth and act on it that produce observable outcomes. The feeding of the five thousand (Matthew 14:13–21) demonstrates this quite plainly: immediate hunger is alleviated, care is demonstrated, and social harmony is momentarily strengthened through shared need (James 1907). Healing the blind, lame, and sick (Luke 4:40; Matthew 9:27–31) also shows tangible, measurable benefits from intervention. From a pragmatic perspective, these acts constitute effectiveness: given human suffering, they mitigate suffering in real-world and daily living.

However, Jesus' ministry extends beyond the immediate utility of the action. Jesus' teachings surrounding love, forgiveness, and self-sacrifice, conveyed especially in the Sermon on the Mount, challenge the ordinary understanding of utility (Matthew 5–7). For example, turning the other cheek or loving an enemy may be conceivable, but they seem distinctly inefficient in a competitive, self-interested world. A somewhat narrow pragmatism may question utility altogether. Nonetheless, we see the long-term value of these teachings as they contribute to trust within relationships, as well as moral value, and community (Peirce 1878; Dewey 1938). In other words, the true "work" of these actions unfolds over time, producing ethical and spiritual qualities that are only partly ascertainable by measurements of success or productivity.

Jesus' call to follow as disciples also creates challenges to the conventional measuring of utility. Leaving family, vocation, and security (Matthew 4:18–22; Luke 9:23–24) could seem inefficient and decidedly irrational from a worldly perspective. The narrative of each suggested that this leaving was for the sake of investing in the Kingdom of God, leading to a transformation of character, ethical discernment, and a disposition toward purpose in God's mission. In light of this observation, pragmatism must be broadened: true effectiveness represents a condition involving observable outcomes and an enduring moral and spiritual outcome (Tillich 1951; Wright 2006).

Practical acts of Jesus were often accompanied by teaching, illustrating their lessons in concrete ways. Notable parables—such as the sower planting seeds (Matthew 13:1–23), and the shepherd seeking a lost sheep (Luke 15:3–7)—are lessons that were pragmatic in their application, while offering supra-pragmatic insight. They uncover truths that are abstract yet grounded in contemporary and observable realities, and also extend beyond those realities to establish morality, relationships, and spiritual meaning in areas beyond tangible sight. Such pedagogical approaches demonstrate that practical actions or interventions, when combined with teaching, can have a cumulative effect for the benefit of students.

For a reader today, Jesus' pragmatic approach may offer a corrective method for tendencies to overvalue efficiency, measurable success, or short-term gain. Practicing and following Him involves specific engagement in living towards the result, but also through an ethical complexity, relational depth, and ultimate purpose for life. Observed results made a difference, but visible outcomes are never separate from the long view of life for moral and spiritual enactment (James 1907; Dewey 1938). Jesus' practical ministry serves as an example of this broader understanding of holistic pragmatism: effectiveness must be interpreted, not only in what can be seen, but in what can be lived, transformed, and aligned with meaning.

Pragmatism and the Cost of Discipleship

Although Jesus' ministry provides benefits that can be seen, he nevertheless repeatedly calls into question a pragmatic worldview that assumes useful is equivalent to convenient or immediately useful. In Luke 9:23-24, Jesus says: "If anyone desires to come after Me, let him deny himself, and take up his cross daily, and follow Me. For whoever desires to save his life will lose it, but whoever loses his life for My sake will save it". To the practical person, bearing a cross or practicing self-denying altruism is ineffective, or even irrational, at least from a reasoned, utilitarian perspective. There are no immediate, definable benefits, but an array of visible, immediate, and measurable costs in the physical, personal, social, and emotional spheres. Yet, if we take these same outcomes from Jesus' perspective, all, or at least many of Jesus' initiatives, accomplish wonderful, worthwhile, and immeasurable outcomes: they build spiritual stamina, moral clarity, and alignment with a transcendent destiny/emotion/decision/reason (James 1907; Tillich 1951).

Modern culture generally measures success by tangible gain, efficiency, or material progress. Jesus interacts and operates in a world of orders of rationality and forms of pragmatism that suggest the most productive and meaningful results of dedicating one's life or resources may not immediately manifest or be contrary to the constructs of usefulness in pragmatic, or conventional, measures of effectiveness. Following Jesus can mean facing economic loss, relational disruption, or social exclusion in both society and personal relationships. Yet, there is no question these costs produce lasting benefits: character formation, empathy development, and the relocation of alignment to a deep value, the Kingdom (of God). The paradox lies at the heart of everyday ethical teaching; true effectiveness is not in a worldly, fictitious way, but as ordered by the alignment of action with timeless principles (Dewey 1938; Wright 2006).

Consider what is observed in the process of Jesus and the rich young ruler (Matthew 19:16-22). By standard pragmatic reasoning, the observance of the Law and moral behavior should produce an outcome that is measured effectively socially and spiritually. Jesus exemplifies a higher-order pragmatism: the abandonment of possessions or materially adjacent relational commitments to God yields measurable outputs that extend beyond merely replacing material goods or achieving immediate satisfaction. There is indeed a quantifiable cost to losing material goods, as well as a transformed consciousness that transcends conventional description and is akin to spiritual transformation. This efficacy, however, cannot be administered or gauged through conventional pragmatic measures (Peirce 1878; James 1907).

Jesus' instruction and expectation of loving one's enemies (Matthew 5:43-48) is another example of practical pragmatism in practice, by calculating our normal computations of reciprocal and mutual advantage. In practical terms, loving one's enemy may be a pragmatic invitation to further pain, deception, or exploitation. Yet, it can create ethical and relational outcomes that shape community, cultivate moral evolution, and advance human relational flourishing. Pragmatism, in a standard or narrow sense, cannot measure these costs or outcomes or expectations much beyond the immanence of experience and anticipated static outcomes; Jesus expands a reconceptualization of measuring effectiveness, with outcomes that exceed the bounds of immediate relational, ethical, and spiritual dimensions, where pragmatism cannot speak or account (Tillich 1951; Wright 2006).

For readers in today's world, the new perspective of pragmatism offers a disciplined and guiding aspect. Efficiency, measurable outcomes, and interim results are culturally validated pragmatics, but they are insufficient evaluation levels for evaluative ethical and spiritual action from a life and personal perspective. Following Jesus is, in fact, learning to view usefulness not only as measurable interim outcomes that are observable, but also as a use and usefulness that can be measured in the interest of aligning with everlasting principles, integrity towards others, and moral authenticity. For this reason, following Jesus is an example of a rational and practical pragmatism that acknowledges the complex nuances of sacrifice and morality, and is, in itself, a whole different story. With this model, Jesus challenges modern assumptions while remaining rigorously practical in a more profound sense.

Pragmatism and Modern Application

Pragmatism pervades almost every domain in contemporary society: business, technology, education, politics, and even self-improvement are now largely preoccupied by measurable results, efficiency, and short-term usefulness. Success is often defined as profit, productivity, or some immediately useful product. In this world, following Jesus may seem impractical or counterintuitive; his teachings invite a reevaluation of the calculations of gain or loss utilized within pragmatism, calculations that consider ethical, relational, or even spiritual results as either as important as short-term results or perhaps even more important (Dewey 1938; James 1907). Jesus' life is an embodied example of practical action interspersed with a visionary perspective: feeding the 5,000 (Matthew 14:13-21) addresses an immediate physical need, but it also exemplifies communal care, creates incentives for generosity, and fosters trust and discipleship over time (Wright 2006). Caring for the sick is an act of compassion that creates physiological changes, but also communicates a deeper ethic in the long run: the value of human dignity, the existence of divine care, and an ethical obligation to act in response to human suffering. We cannot explain or justify these actions through pragmatic understandings; they work in the moment but have the potential to be transformative across relational, moral, and spiritual planes (Tillich 1951).

Contemporary readers can engage with the dual aspects of decision-making, leadership, and everyday living. In business or political spheres, decisions based on efficiency or profit may yield measurable results, but they may also minimize ethical costs, create relational distrust, or overlook the longer-term outcomes of pragmatism. Jesus' teachings offer a broader heuristic: rather than simply evaluating the instantaneous results or immediate impact, weigh the results in light of practical wisdom, ethical integrity, human flourishing, and long-term change. Pragmatism is necessary, but it is inadequate; the first brings additive characteristics to pragmatism (Peirce 1878; James 1907).

Moreover, contemporary culture often defines "success" in terms of short-term results, such as status, social capital, or immediate gratification. Jesus shifts the consideration of success, indicating that decisions aligned with holistic principles, relational trust, and accountability, as well as moral obligation, are costly for these very reasons, but also significant in long-term and lasting ways. The paradox inspires readers to integrate measurable usefulness and perseverance using ethical, relational, and spiritual wisdom, ultimately growing their understanding of practical wisdom (Tillich 1951; Wright 2006).

A contemporary expression of Jesus' teachings is a reframing of pragmatism. Action is essential, but its value is best understood through a more holistic and deeper framework of meaningful human existence, moral depth, and spiritual coherence. In embracing pragmatism, readers can connect their decision-making across contemporary issues with ethical considerations, a relational view of the world, and a transcendent purpose. Jesus' wisdom remains useful, disruptive, and pragmatically transformative for Christians, as well as for constructions of post-modern ethical wisdom in the twenty-first century (Dewey 1938; Wright 2006).

Pragmatism, Short-Term Gain, and Eternal Significance

Without critically reflecting on the term 'pragmatism,' it can quickly shift to a form of utilitarianism, where actions are considered based only on immediate benefit, convenience, and efficiency. As a society, we often consider this form of "pragmatism" to be practical. It

47

might even shape our sense of personal ambition, our organizational strategies, our work ethics, and even our religious practices. People often become devoted to a philosophy, pursue an education, or engage in a faith practice, not simply because of a process of exploration, but rather the measurable and concrete benefits that the choices yield. Yet throughout Jesus' teachings as a whole, there is a quasi-continuous struggle against this restricted form of success or pragmatic purpose. Jesus seems to indicate that the ultimate value and fulfillment may necessitate sacrifice or some form of delayed gratification, rather than a pragmatic and immediate form of utility (James 1907; Wright 2006).

Jesus' admonition to take up one's cross (Luke 9:23) is again a recognizable example of the tension between pragmatic evaluation and the deeper logic of the Kingdom of God. Denial of self, service to others, or ethical and moral standards might seem ridiculous or impractical if evaluated from a worldly perspective. Yet, each of these behaviors may be a crucial part of Jesus' definition of success, where "success" is framed in terms of an ongoing process of transformation, alignment, and contribution to the flourishing of humanity and the world throughout the values found in the Kingdom of God (Tillich, 1951; Dewey, 1938). The understanding of ideal usefulness moves beyond the realm of visibility: actions are not considered "useful" based on visible results, but by their capacity to educate character, develop community, or advance a deeper value that can last over the ages of time.

Modern readers battle against this challenge as well. A corporate leader may prioritize profit over responsible practice and application; an educator may value grades or information gathering over critical thinking; a person may prioritize their comfort or recognition over the integrity of relationships and spiritual well-being. Pragmatism alone cannot judge the decision made here and now, or the longer future ramifications on the interconnected web of being or practice in life. Following the logic or model of Jesus shows that practical action can only be fully manifested in meaning when it is grounded in moral perception or insight, relational perceptiveness, or some vision that considers beyond the act being evaluated. A little bit of tension is not misplaced by accepting the idea that this logic may be counterintuitive: giving freely, serving others, forgiving, and loving even our enemies, who do not fit conventional utilitarian principles, have more productive power for a longer-lasting impact (Wright, 2006; Tillich, 1951).

The tension between pragmatism and supra-pragmatic principles allows for balance in our current contemporary life. It remains practical for the work of healing, teaching, feeding, and innovating. Each of these actions can remain in the framework of what is "practical." Still, these characteristics are pitted against the ideas of eternal significance, ethical coherence, and depth of relationship for informed decision-making and choices. Decisions may not seem practical in the short run, but they can have life-altering consequences that can mean everything to the individual or community (James, 1907; Peirce, 1878).

The teaching, actions, and example of Jesus frame the pragmatic lens. Jesus affirms practical actions while at the same time reshaping the parameters of for work in life. Real effectiveness, in this vision of order, is not simply measured in the short term but rather comes through duration, ethical characteristics, and the transcendence of some form of purpose. The logic of the Kingdom of God can be quite challenging and counter to modern practice thought. Yet, it exhibits a model of action that is real and transformative in a world driven by short-term commitments or utilitarianism (Dewey, 1938; Wright, 2006).

Pragmatism and Shallow Christianity

Pragmatism, as a philosophical perspective, poses a simple question: Does it work? In contemporary life, this one question dominates our decision-making processes in professional, social, and even spiritual contexts. When we fail to analyze faith through a pragmatic lens, it can lead to a conditional, instrumental, or transactional form of Christianity. In such a faith, one can disclose one's commitment to the faith primarily to receive some personally beneficial good. The benefits, often characterized by long-term ethical and spiritual benefits, can range from health to wealth, personal status, and even the comfort of knowing we have our own kind of "covenant." Pragmatism, as an unexamined approach to life generally and to our faith specifically, can obscure the relational richness and depth of moral formation embodied by Jesus (James, 1907; Wright, 2006).

The Gospels provide the starkest examples of this pragmatic distortion. In Matthew 19:16-24, Jesus encounters a rich young ruler who seeks to confirm his status regarding eternal life. This young man asks Jesus, What shall I do to inherit eternal life? Yet, when he is told to sell everything, his faith serves as a means to maintain his material comfort. His faith in Jesus is functional to faith, but it is not a response to the transformative ethical life Jesus models. Jesus turns the young man upside down by asserting that real discipleship is not just a function of utility or speed of favorable outcomes. This is not to say the kingdom of God is simply a service contract for predictable outcomes, but to understand the very contours of what it is to be, i.e., the radical reorientation of values, priorities, and identity (Tillich 1951; Dewey 1938).

For the twenty-first-century reader, the concept and lived experience of faith in Jesus hold special relevance. We live in a society that increasingly measures "success" and "effectiveness" in terms of short-term, quantifiable, observable outcomes. Our lives, and indeed modern expressions of faith, filtered through the lens of pragmatism, will develop a similar posture: we would likely follow Jesus radically, but only to the extent that it alleviates some discomfort or results in tangible outcomes. However, a pragmatic approach cannot begin to account for the multidimensionality of human life, the ethical perplexities of relational living, and, in the face of opposing views, the endless significance of moral and ethical growth (Lewis 1952; Wright 2006).

Jesus' critique exposes a shallow, transactional faith, revealing a principle that transcends previous definitions of temporal pragmatism. Jesus continually invites us to reflection, greater ethical vigilance, and even atonement for relational engagement, showing us that some of the most meaningful things we experience are not immediately agreed upon, and are not fundamentally measurable by our typically mundane definitions of outcomes. Suppose one measures one's faith solely in terms of prevailing favorable practical benefits. In that case, they risk neglecting character formation and moral responsibility. In today's terms, we would warn against an "ROI" driven spirituality, approaching human experience as simple +++/—- equations, and limiting moral complexity to simple calculations and advantage (James 1907; Peirce 1878).

Here, we view Jesus not as an idealized, timeless figure doling out land slogans but rather as a radical realist whose life and teaching force us to engage in pragmatic thinking, only to expose its limits. In many respects, as unexamined pragmatism would allow, a shallow Christianity in response is not enough. Jesus, too, provides a way forward, once the meaning of usefulness is redefined: the most "effective" acts are those that are more aligned with justice, integrity, and the longer-term flourishing of people and whole communities. Grounding the Gospel in lived experience, while providing historical context and a contemporary vantage point to understand modern worldviews, this section will unpack a pragmatic faith-based framework that is both demanding and enduring in its meaning, far exceeding the definitions upon which it was based.

True Success Beyond Immediate Gain

Traditionally, pragmatism values effectiveness based on observable, immediate results. We know business effectiveness based on profit, education is effective based on performance on tests, and government effectiveness is measured based on efficiency. When applied to spiritual or ethical life, pragmatism evaluates an act's effectiveness based on observable gains, such as wealth, health, social acceptance, and personal comfort. However, the Gospels tend to provide a different measurement for meaningful action. Jesus is consistently re-orienting what it means to "succeed" or be effective in action (James 1907; Wright 2006).

Actions such as feeding the five thousand (Matthew 14:13-21) and healing the blind and lame (Mark 8:22-26) can be easily described as "effective" based on observable results: hunger is relieved, suffering is alleviated, and dignity is restored to an individual. Nevertheless, the teaching of Jesus indicates that these "successful" acts will never be effective solely based on observable outcomes—they point to a greater reality, the Kingdom of God, and the long-term change of hearts, relationships, and community. Pragmatic evaluation in isolation might celebrate the immediate outcome of relief from hunger or observable improvement. Still, pragmatic evaluation without more substantial insight misses the evaluation of action in moral, relational, and spiritual terms (Lewis 1952; Tillich 1951).

This disparity between the future usefulness of an action and its lasting weight in experience is central to meaningfully engaging with

Jesus in practical life. The moral insight, relational richness, and eternal consequences of every action will often escape our conventional measures of "effectiveness." For example, feeding the hungry may alleviate the physical concern of hunger, and in doing so, anticipates and embodies compassion, shared belonging, and affirms the value of human life. Healing the sick returns the sick to the agency. It embodies and anticipates moral and spiritual qualities of truth, including empathy, mercy, and divine care. Outcomes of human agency won't be immediately measurable but will reflect a deeper accounting of effectiveness anchored in fostered expectations (Dewey 1938; Peirce 1878).

Success, as measured by Jesus, is never without moral integrity, richness of relational interaction, and alignment with God's purposes. A pragmatic framework may view the death of Christ as a failure, suffering as inefficient, or an act of generosity that includes self-sacrifice as a waste. Yet the actions of Jesus and those aligned with God's purpose all carry weight that extends beyond and through empirical evidence to the realm of experience. Eternal life, reconciliation, and moral transformation become the ultimate measure of effectiveness, serving as benchmarks for the combination of practicality with moral and relational integrity standards (Wright 2006; Tillich 1951).

For contemporary readers, this perspective of our vocation with Jesus reorders effectiveness. Pragmatism is not rejected; instead, pragmatism is reordered: effectiveness is measurable and observable in practical ways, but it must conform to ultimate purposes. The success of effectiveness encompasses not only immediate effectiveness but also insight into morals, relational integrity, and spiritual impact over time. In this sense, the teachings of Jesus move pragmatism away from a transactional assessment of usefulness toward a framework for service with a practical foundation and enduring intention (James 1907; Lewis 1952).

Modern Application of Pragmatic Faith

Pragmatism now reigns in nearly every aspect of modern life: corporate strategy, technological development, public policy, education, and even lifestyle choices are so often considered in terms of utility, measurability, and results. This contemporary way of thinking asks the questions: Does it work? Does it address the need? Does it result in anything? In this environment, faith can find itself under the weight of trying to prove its worth in terms of usefulness, specifically in terms of finite, immediate benefits, such as physical healing, personal prosperity, social influence, or personal fulfillment. The life and teachings of Jesus open up space for a far richer engagement, where useful action must also engage with moral, relational, and historical sensibilities, but it must also provide an orientation that is more than practical value.

Jesus' life demonstrates that useful, pragmatic action can be both immediate and lasting. The feeding of the 5,000 serves an immediate purpose of addressing hunger (Matt 14:13-21), but ultimately, it also directs attention to the deeper significance of spiritual nourishment, communal support, and moral responsibility. The same can be said for healing and teaching: the observable or measurable outcomes matter, yet these procedures also carry with them an ethical and relational referral that transcends the observable or measurable. The useful or pragmatic outcome of an action is closely tied to its ethical and relational consequences. A measurable purpose or pragmatic function is important, but insufficient in the full picture of what an ethical, human action accomplishes.

Bringing this into contemporary life would require us to recalibrate our understanding of pragmatism, or the practical approach to problem-solving. In a business context, for example, success is not just summed up in predictable aspects of profit, but also considers social responsibility, employee well-being, and ethical business models. In education, efficacy certainly matters, but it is not summed up in terms of standardized testing alone; it also encompasses moral formation, civic engagement, and the relational element of education. While technology provides efficiency and makes the mundane convenient, it also raises questions about ethical and societal implications, as well as whether it showcases our best as humans. So when we think of pragmatism, or faith without pragmatism, we are not saying it is anti-efficiency or that we should not consider measurable results; instead, we are suggesting that measurable, functional outcomes can be understood, believed, and acted upon while being a part of an extended engagement with lasting values, moral insight, and relational coherence.

Furthermore, applying pragmatic faith in contemporary life entails the deliberate engagement with and integration of supra-rational elements. Rationality, evidence, outcomes, and social implications still matter—they guide both rational and social accountability—and also require us to consider long-term implications, ethical engagement, and social implications. Thus, we would understand practical effectiveness in the world by how it performs in relation to enduring moral, spiritual, and societal values. As such, faith should not be either irrational or escapist; instead, faith naturally engages the world in disciplined, relational awareness of all things and weighs what does work against what ultimately matters.

Pragmatic faith in the twenty-first century is often anti-reductionistic. It assumes that measurable, applicable achievement and ethical existence can coexist. All said, actions grounded in love, justice, and relational care can be both valuable and consequential. As we understand Jesus' life and teachings, pragmatism can be enriched, but not replaced: the useful outcomes can become a bridge to eternal significance, ethical depth, and relational flourishing, thus demonstrating that faith can still have relevance, realism, and transformation in a pragmatic world.

Chapter Four

Scientism: When Science Becomes a God

The Meaning of Scientism

Scientism refers to the belief that science has the greatest—or only—access to truth, placing experience and natural laws above other ways of knowing. While science itself is a disciplined method for studying the natural world, scientism extends this approach into a comprehensive worldview, claiming that empirical inquiry alone can answer questions of meaning, moral obligations, and purpose (Harris 2010; Pigliucci 2012). This approach, however, can overlook aspects of human experience, ethics, and relational knowledge that cannot be fully measured or accounted for in observable phenomena.

With this in mind, the historical context of scientism can be traced back to the Scientific Revolution and rationalism of the Enlightenment. As philosophers like Galileo, Newton, and Bacon paved the way for systematic inquiry into science with methods of observation, experimentation, and reasoning, the success of these methods of inquiry gave rise to a larger cultural assumption: empiricism is the sole source of truth. By the 19th and 20th centuries, this perspective of experiential truth, harvested through the scientific method, expanded from not just natural science but also into philosophy, ethics, and public policy, embedding epistemic and ethical assumptions surrounding knowledge, progress, and what contributes to human flourishing (Shapin 1996; Feyerabend 1975).

In the modern 21st century, characterized by data analytics, machine learning, and technological innovation, scientism remains the dominant paradigm in public discourse and decision-making. This culture, valuing experience and observable outcomes over either/or relationships or reflective purpose, now dominates exchanges of every kind. As a result, it continues to append enormous significance to the conclusions generated through the scientific method, but commentators of our epistemological age caution, while empiricism holds great explanatory power of our physical and natural world, not all questions of meaning and moral obligations, or of the nature of reality can always be considered through the lens of observable data or things or matter (Nagel 2012; Sagan 1996).

Jesus' Counterpoint to Scientism

The Gospels show a competing engagement with reality. Jesus, as portrayed in the Gospels of Matthew, Mark, Luke, and John, combines keen observation of human life with the moral and spiritual insights derived from that observation. He speaks into the observable world while simultaneously revealing its ethical and transcendent dimensions. For example, in Matthew 6:25–27, he observes the birds of the air and the lilies of the field, using these examples to unpack truths about providence and human worth that extend beyond the empirical measurement of the birds' migration or the lilies' petals. Likewise, in John 4:13–14, Jesus describes living water to the woman at the well, linking physical thirst to spiritual satisfaction—a truth not accessible through data or experiment alone. These observations reflect that while observation is useful, it is not adequate for capturing the fullness of human life and purpose (Wright 2006; Lewis 1952).

From a modern perspective, Jesus' approach disrupts the limits of scientism, but does not reject reason or evidence. He acknowledges the world as it is—observable, tangible, and real—while pointing, from there, to moral, relational, and spiritual realities. The Kingdom of God becomes a vehicle for engaging empirical knowledge in a critical way—not denying what it has to tell us, but noticing its blind spots. There is room for recognizing empirically studied facets of our reality, but the Gospels suggest apprehending life in its fullness requires recognizing ethical meaning, relational liveliness, and ultimate purpose (Colossians 1:16–17; Tillich 1951).

Attending to scientism and the teachings of Jesus reveals the tension in human understanding between the desire to know what is measurable and the need to comprehend what is unquantifiable. Jesus exemplifies radical realism, which insists on the fusion of observation and moral-spiritual knowing, offering a lens for 21st-century readers to understand life and navigate a world of science, technology, and skepticism (Harris 2010; Wright 2006).

Knowledge and Creation

The natural world displays astonishing patterns, order, and consistency, warranting close examination and study. From galaxies to DNA, creation provides a reality that captivates and challenges the human mind. The ability to empirically inquire enables the description of processes, laws, and future consequences in a way that provides a window into the workings of the universe. Although science can demonstrate how things occur, it cannot, by itself, answer the meaning of existence or the ultimate purpose of the world (Sagan 1996; Barrow 2005).

The biblical worldview is explicit that creation is a window into the divine. Psalm 19:1 states, "The heavens declare the glory of God; and the firmament shows His handiwork." Also, Romans 1:20 notes that God's invisible qualities—the eternal power and divine nature—are clearly seen in the things He has made. These verses imply knowledge about the natural world points beyond a mere mechanism, but to a reality filled with moral significance, intention, and design. Creation is not simply a system of laws to be described; it reflects a reality that points to purpose, a "fingerprint" of reality beyond empirical witness (Plantinga 2011; Polkinghorne 2005).

Alongside this, modern scientism tends to describe these experiences as self-existing or an accident. Complexity, beauty, and order are simply features of natural selection, chance, or some physical law, as all meaning, moral purpose, and ultimate destiny would lie outside the inquiry (Pigliucci 2012; Harris 2010). Although these ideas may provide some useful understanding, they may not answer questions such as why existence exists, what constitutes human flourishing, or whether life has a moral orientation.

Following the life of Jesus shows the limits of empiricism and reveals how revelation enters into the observable. His miracles, for example, turning water into wine, walking on the sea, and feeding the multitudes, were visible in observable laws (John 2:1–11; Matthew 14:13–21). The teachings of Jesus connect the observable and earthly to eternal principles, where human action and understanding intersect with moral and spiritual connections. Central to the Gospels, the resurrection invites credence that ultimate reality cannot be observed through empirical methods in ways that do not involve significance of meaning, destiny, and relational truth that transcends measurement or prediction (1 Corinthians 15:3–8).

From a modern cultural perspective, the interaction between science and scripture highlights a tension that is particularly visible today. Rational inquiry provides a reliable method for exploring mechanisms in creation; however, without further consideration of the moral and spiritual dimensions, rational inquiry could reduce life to a purely material universe. The biblical witness, in contrast, situates empirical observations in a meaningful and purposeful reality that demonstrates that knowledge of creation must involve a reflection of meaning, moral order, and ultimate reality (Wright 2006; Polkinghorne 2005).

In this way, relating to creation provides a model for how Jesus speaks to the modern mind, where reason and empirical observations are valued, while pointing beyond to meaning. Knowledge and discovery are not antithetical to spiritual existence; rather, the lived experience is situated within a greater vision that involves the natural world as a testimony to God's glory in a meaningful and purposeful world with a moral life.

61

Jesus as Truth Beyond Measurement

In today's environment, dominated by a culture of scientism, there is a tendency to view truth broadly in terms of what is observable, measurable, and reproducible. Consequently, facts verified by experiment or data are privileged. At the same time, issues of meaning, ethics, or purpose are often left as secondary or subjective considerations. Within the context of this framework, knowledge is equated with measurable information, and reality is considered only when it can be proven or calculated (Pigliucci 2012; Harris 2010). Timeless truths, as propounded in the Gospels, present a radically different understanding of truth in Jesus. "I am the way, the truth, and the life" (John 14:6) declares Jesus, which places Him as the truth itself, not a knowledge base or one of the innumerable perspectives of many. Truth, in this sense, is relational, moral, historical, and spiritual. It cannot be fully exported to a lab, encoded into a dataset, or transcribed into an algorithm (Wright 2006; Plantinga 2011).

Truth for Jesus is incarnational: it is embodied in a human life, lived in time, observable in experience, yet beyond all empirical measures. His teaching, parables, and acts demonstrate principles that can be documented and observed, yet the full embodiment and weight of meaning these acts signify reach even beyond that which can be quantified. For example, the Sermon on the Mount (Matthew 5-7) is an exposé of ethical truths and relational prescriptions revealed through lived experience. This is relevant in understanding reality beyond mere external experiences and observations; it involves the realities of human hearts, intention, and moral decisions (Foster 2018).

Jesus' truth is therefore relational and moral, shaping and transcending our assumptions of a solo moral, reductive, and purely empirical reality. Human understanding, he implies, necessitates some integration of intellect, ethics, and historical awareness. Truth is not merely a list of data points to be filed; it is how we humans cohere or participate in God's redemptive purposes, how we engage with lives of moral reality, and how we navigate through the temporal and spiritual experiences of living. Paul observes that "in Him are hidden all the treasures of wisdom and knowledge" (Colossians 2:3). Ultimate understanding is to be found relationally, not simply empirically.

This understanding of truth presents an important challenge to modern readers. There is value to empirical knowledge and rational inquiry; however, their limits are equally essential to highlight. Scientific observation can and does explore the description of natural processes. Still, it does not ascertain moral obligation, ultimate meaning, or adequacy of human destiny. Jesus embodies a truth that encompasses observational experience, ethical engagement, and spiritual insight, serving as a holistic framework for viewing lived reality (Polkinghorne 2005; Barrow 2005). In the effort to demonstrate Jesus as truth within this relational and moral framework, it is incumbent upon us to address the challenges posed by the contemporary tendency to equate knowledge solely with measurement. Jesus' truth challenges the notion of active agency in authentic understanding and advocates for a threshold scope that prioritizes the relational human experience, grounded in the historical morality of the ethical dimensions of people's lives. This understanding suggests the very presence of truth, as observed in his way of ultimate transcendence, calling readers to engage in relationships with reality, integrating reason, ethics, and awareness of spiritual beliefs.

The Resurrection and the Limits of Natural Law

The resurrection of Jesus presents a significant challenge to the assumptions of a purely naturalistic or scientistic worldview. While empirical observation and the laws of biology and physics function as systems for understanding the natural world, the resurrection is an event that transcends systems. As noted in the Gospels, Jesus' resurrection is described as a historic event that occurred after his crucifixion, witnessed by several people over time (Luke 24:1–12; 1 Corinthians 15:3–8) (Habermas 2003; Wright).

For contemporary scientific perspectives, which equate truth with quantifiable and reproducible phenomena—including natural laws, natural processes, and natural causal relationships—the resurrection represents a counter-experience. Natural law operates within observable and predictable parameters; that is, it describes the ways things can occur and interact, as well as the sustained outcomes to which we can observe and eventually replicate. But the resurrection violates natural law. It may help set the parameters of decay, of biology, and of physical causation. Still, science is unable to determine that a person who died on a particular day at a particular time resurrected after three days. Any reduction of the resurrection to myth, metaphor, or psychological experience is a concession of the limits of perspective that restricts realities from occurring outside of empirical verification (McGrath 2011; Geisler & Turek 2004).

Still, the Gospels aim to present the resurrection as more than an anomaly. Resurrection has moral, relational, and spiritual implications. Those who witnessed this event began to construct alternative understandings of their lives and purpose, as well as the destiny of all humanity, along the lines of understanding fear, awe, and transformative conviction. The resurrection suggests that the extreme limit of reality cannot be limited to what can be measured, counted, or predicted. Rather, as Acts 2:24 notes, God "raised Him up, having loosed the pangs of death, because it was not possible that He should be held by it." The resurrection signals authority over the natural order, revealing dimensions of truth, justice, and purpose that transcend the empirical world and its observational limits.

From the perspective of analysis, the resurrection opens the possibility for a wider understanding of knowledge and evidence. Knowledge of the historical development of moral and non-moral leaders of the time, as well as spiritual cognition, becomes complementary and essential to observation and experimentation. The event provides an example that engages empirical facts (the crucifixion, burial, and empty tomb) with relational and ethical (and transcendent) truths. Thus, the resurrection provides a model for engaging the modern mind by affirming thought and evidence while expressing to that mind that ultimate meaning exceeds the outcome that science might establish (Craig 2000; Licona 2010).

The theological and philosophical implications are important. The resurrection suggests that observation, as a means of understanding the natural world, if important, is not a solution to ultimate reality. In constructing a total account of being human, historical events, moral transformations, and spiritual insight must be considered. The resurrection of Jesus embodies a radical realism. Yes, it is a historical event that requires measurable, observable outcomes in individual human lives, but it is also an event that transcends natural law to reveal a reality and experience of divine purpose, moral authority, and transcendent truth (Habermas 2003; Wright 2003).

Reflecting on the resurrection in terms of "scientism" reveals a persistent tension in modern thought. On the one hand, the outcome provides a significant avenue for insight into the structure of the universe and its presumed workings. On the other hand, experiences like the resurrection demonstrate that authority, reality, and meaning cannot be presumed to be confined to experiences determined by empirical limits. The tension of the resurrection presents an invitation to conceive the ordinary, and in the case of the resurrection — the ultimate —as an invitation to engage in observation, historical inquiry, and ethical-spiritual reflection to gain a more meaningful account of life, truth, and purpose.

Modern Implications of Scientism and Faith

The modern world is increasingly rooted in empirical logic, data-informed decision-making, and technological advancement. The terms artificial intelligence, predictive analytics, and evidence-informed politics embody a worldview that prioritizes measurable results and observable phenomena as primary measures of truth. Scientism is a dominant perspective in the public sphere, education, and government, which foregrounds reality up to what can be measured or established by some empirical test (McGrath 2011; Polanyi 1962). Consequently, this valuing of evidence has advanced knowledge and efficiency, but often placed issues of moral obligation, meaning, and human purpose on the sidelines.

The biblical witness seeks to provide a corrective and a complement. Jesus' teachings suggest a framework that transcends the scientific, which values observation, rational understanding, and empirical insight, but does not rest there as if it is a complete understanding of reality. For example, in Matthew 16:26, He asks, "For what profit is it to a man if he gains the whole world, and loses his own soul?" As a rhetorical question, the expectation is to understand the limits of material, measurable successes without ethical, relational, and spiritual awareness. Likewise, Proverbs 3:19-20 remarks, "The Lord by wisdom founded the earth; by understanding He established the heavens; by His knowledge the depths were broken up, and clouds dropped down the dew", suggesting creation itself reveals a more integrated order of observable things along with purpose, morality, and divine purpose. In practical terms, Jesus' model invites interaction with the visible world without reducing it to a mechanistic explanation. Technology, AI, and empirical knowledge are effective tools in understanding complexity, providing human flourishing, and discovering order in the universe. However, at some point, decisions related to ethics, public policy, and cultural inquiry will need to integrate relational, moral, and existential realities, spaces where scientism cannot provide guidance, if the concept of guidance can even be applied (Geisler and Turek, 2004; Craig, 2000). Faith, for now, is not a dismissal of rational inquiry and empirical knowledge, but a context within which to locate inquiries and the understanding of human life and human purpose.

Jesus' life represents this integration. Jesus teaches, recognizes the power of miracles, and makes ethical proclamations that reveal empirical reality and moral-spiritual discernment simultaneously. The miracle of the feeding of the five thousand (John 6: 1-14), for example, implies an attunement to material realities, such as hunger, resources, and distribution, but is also meant to reveal deeper truths about provision, compassion, and trust. Jesus' interaction with social and religious structures also demonstrates that understanding social systems, observing and measuring patterns, and exercising rational thought are necessary, but these must always be oriented toward processes related to justice, mercy, and anything ultimately meaningful (Matt 23:23).

From a modern perspective, the implications are clear—while scientism provides enormous power in accessing and acting toward comprehension, it also cannot attend to anything of ultimate significance. Jesus models a brand of radical realism in which empirical observation, rational thought, and technology are understood in the context of moral and spiritual discernment. It involves a way of thinking in which knowledge and faith are not pitted against each other; instead, they work interdependently, leading humans to navigate an increasingly complex world while understanding eternal and relational realities (Habermas, 2003; Wright, 2003).

Engaging with scientism today means embracing it as a valuable contributor to life, while not allowing it to dominate the truth and human reality. Jesus portrays a way of employing a holistic understanding of reality, which requires a simultaneous experience of both observation and moral insight, empirical rigor and moral discernment, as well as measurable knowing and relational-spiritual knowing, understanding faith and reason in this way, as we together attempt to engage with "scientific" life in a technologically driven contemporary society.

Chapter Five

NIHILISM: THE VOID AND THE LIGHT

*I*n its most popular form today, nihilism holds that life lacks meaning. Philosophical, existential, and cultural articulations of that view generally emphasize the human experience of finitude, the lack of ultimate meaning, and the arbitrary nature of values (Nietzsche, 1887; Camus, 1942). Contemporary literature, art, and media often convey a pervasive sense of malaise, portraying life as a saga of struggle, futility, and fleetingness. In many ways, nihilism represents the intellectual and emotional landscape into which Jesus' message enters the world.

This nominally representational struggle of human longing for meaning in the face of an empty existence is present even within the Scriptures themselves. The book of Ecclesiastes begins with the stark observation, "Vanity of vanities, says the Preacher, vanity of vanities! All is vanity" (Ecclesiastes 1:2). The writer observes the ceaseless cyclical repetition of nature, labor, and human ambition, and notes their apparent uselessness. This experience of existential emptiness resonates with nihilistic thought today, where empirical knowledge, technological progress, and cultural development frequently leave one still unsatisfied in their existential search for meaning.

Into this world of despair, Jesus provides a compelling vision. He states, "I have come that they may have life, and that they may have it more abundantly" (John 10:10). Here, life is relativized to a relational experience, a purposeful course of action, and an eternal breath that transcends observable impacts or temporal achievements. Nihilism evaluates existence based on external accomplishments or what we can observe for ourselves, to see if it stands the test of time. In contrast, Jesus locates meaning in the unseen, in moral and spiritual realities, and in the continuity of God's purpose. And the abundance He promises involves ethical responsibility, relational depth, and the anticipation of everlasting significance. The cross as a paradox. On the surface, Jesus' death may suggest nihilism is validated: a victim of execution, humiliated, and defeated, it represents human experience as suffering, injustice, and death. But it is only through resurrection that this apparent gap is made whole with ultimate significance. On the cross and resurrection, it is demonstrated that what seemed so final and without purpose could be shaped by God's purpose. As Paul writes in Romans 8:18, "For I consider that the sufferings of this present time are not worthy to be compared with the glory which shall be revealed in us". The ultimate victory over death means our suffering can be reframed with meaning that contrasts with nihilism.

In the current culture, we see this tension play out with a pervasive experience of despair, alienation, and existential questions, suggesting the relevance of nihilism in our time as well. Nihilism offers an analytical understanding of the fragility and impermanence of human life, but leaves moral and relational purposes unaddressed, ultimately providing only a void. Jesus' message addresses this gap without denying reality, acknowledging real suffering, mortality, and the limits of human power, to convey a framework where meaning, hope, and purpose are real and attainable.

From a modern perspective, the wrestling between nihilism and the Gospel demonstrates a radical realism in Jesus. Jesus does not deny the void nor replace it with some abstract ideals. Jesus enters the void, transforms it, and offers a pathway to an enduring and relational life that is abundant. Jesus addresses a cultural and existential longing for significance by demonstrating that, even in a world filled with despair, there is still light, hope, and ultimate meaning to be found in our relationships and lives (Plantinga 2000; Wright 2003).

Nihilism in Modern Thought

Nihilism is commonly described as a philosophical viewpoint that holds life lacks inherent meaning, purpose, or worth. It highlights that there are no objective moral principles, ultimate ends, or transcendental meaning, often indicating that human existence is contingent, transient, or even the consequence of an accident (Nietzsche 1887; Camus 1942). In the nihilist view, actions, accomplishments, and the efforts of morality may ultimately be all for nothing, perpetuating an extreme sense of emptiness for the individual. Philosophers like Friedrich Nietzsche have intensely critiqued traditional religious and moral structures, diagnosed the "death of God," and warned of the despair and lack of certainty that might await humanity in an existence without an ultimate purpose.

In expressing nihilism today, it might be as likely to appear in philosophy, but it has also filtered into literature, art, and commentary on cultural issues. Existential novels often feature characters grappling with meaninglessness, alienation, and the perceived arbitrariness of life. Visual art and film often depict conflicting images of absurdity, despair, and the tenuousness of human endeavors - all pointing to the same collective consciousness that inhabits a cultural awareness of transience and contingency. Even in discussions of science or technology, there can be an element of nihilism when human value is measured strictly in quantitative terms: life is reduced to data points, success is defined by productivity, and worth is primarily assessed in terms of utility, rather than relational, moral, or spiritual value. Nihilism resonates in these instances because it provides an articulation of an implicit sense in the human experience that exists in the universe governed by laws, yet has little assurance of meaning or moral direction (Vattimo 2002; Gray 2007).

Understanding nihilism is especially relevant when considering the dynamic impact of Jesus' teaching in the world today. Here, nihilism finds a relevant place as a contrast to the metaphysical world posited by "scientism," which posits facts and natural laws as the ultimate reality, beyond rational forms of knowledge, and rationalism would prioritize. Nihilism threatens and confronts the human condition, not with knowledge or method, but with a void of existence. Nihilism reveals the fragility of what might be called human hope without a transcendent foundation. Nihilism equally provides the stage by which the relevance of Jesus' teaching can be recognized in stark clarity as referring to the void that life entails — it proposes that life lacks meaning as a way to signal that meaning may not be available to us. So nihilism creates the stage on which the significance of Jesus' impact can be seen in absolute clarity.

The tension nihilism introduces is not abstract; it is highly experiential. Many people have reported feeling alienated, if not lost, in a world of rapid technological change, social upheaval, and global uncertainty. Careers, relationships, and accomplishments, even when objectively assessed, may not fulfill a more profound yearning for meaning or purpose. Those who feel this void will be situated in a context where they engage with the promise of Jesus as offering abundant life (John 10:10), which means that the void exposed by nihilism is to be filled. In this context, Jesus' promise of abundant life offers a new framework where meaning, relational value, and moral grounding may be found, despite all observable evidence of the fragility of existence; life can still be profound.

By placing nihilism in the philosophical and cultural context, it can be grasped the degree of existential tension that Jesus engages. Understanding the broader implications of pervasive despair, alienation, and a sense of meaninglessness is essential to understanding the transformative impact of His life, death, and resurrection. Nihilism is not simply another philosophical abstraction - nor is it a highbrow abstraction - nihilism is a live reality through which the difference between the void and hope in Christ becomes simultaneously clear and compelling.

Biblical Reflections on Human Emptiness

The human experience of longing, frustration, and existential uncertainty is not a postmodern idea. All of Scripture, including the book of Ecclesiastes, acknowledges the tension between human aspiration and the futility of worldly pursuits. Ecclesiastes offers a brooding and introspective examination of the transient nature of life and the limits of human working. As a case in point, the first verse of the book encapsulates the struggle: "Vanity of vanities, says the Preacher, vanity of vanities! All is vanity." (Ecclesiastes 1:2) The

Hebrew word for "vanity" (hebel) means transience, breath, or vapor—a figurative way to describe the elusive and evanescent nature of worldly pursuits.

A recurring theme in the book of Ecclesiastes is the struggle against the reality that labor, knowledge, and pleasure, while pursued earnestly, are inadequate in fulfilling the more profound human longing for meaning. The Preacher observes that toil leads to temporary results, understanding, but does not achieve ultimate meaning, and pleasure fades eventually (Ecclesiastes 1:3; 1:16–18; 2:1–11). Even erudition becomes an object of admiration, but it too cannot ultimately answer questions about meaning and destiny. Kierkegaard stated that anxiety, or existential angst, arises from the lack of tension between finite human striving for meaning and the infinite horizon of meaning—that achievement alone will not suffice the soul (Kierkegaard 1844). Similarly, Tillich expressed that the human spirit strives toward ultimate concern; absence of transcendent concern for what is ultimately significant can lead to existential emptiness (Tillich 1951). The similarity between these observations in the Scriptures and nihilism, as we understand it today, is noteworthy. Modern society equates success with being productive, performing well, or possessing tangible assets that can be measured. Careers, accolades, or technological achievements can distract us briefly, but they never truly meet the deeper human desire for ultimate meaning. The cycles Ecclesiastes noted—the rising and setting of the sun, working for a living, or experiencing knowledge and pleasure—are representative of our modern experience, which strives for accomplishments that do not propel us toward existential answers. Nietzsche's remark about the death of God and the consequent moral vacuum highlights the same tension: lacking any transcendent basis for meaning, human endeavor feels fundamentally futile (Nietzsche 1887).

However, Scripture does not leave us in despair regarding the human condition. By honestly demonstrating the limits of labor, knowledge, and pleasure, the biblical witness presents human longing for purpose as a legitimate and pressing issue. There is a recognition of emptiness that serves to liberate and prepare human beings for the recognition of transcendent meaning, moral obligation, and relational fulfillment. Pascal's musings in Pensées reflect the same dynamic of confronting the void and emptiness, yet aiming one's heart toward God; the human being is either consumed by purely abstract rationalism or empirical calculation (Pascal 1669). In this way, Colleagues and other biblical authors confront the questions raised by nihilism about afflictions, futility, and mortality, only to draw us into an orientation in which we can grapple with these realities rather than ignore them.

From a modern perspective, connecting human emptiness through the lens of Scripture provides both a bridge and a contrast to modern nihilism. It acknowledges the futility while simultaneously creating the conditions for hope and significance. You can recognize that even Solomon—the wisest of men—saw the limits of human effort, which prepares the reader to find Jesus' life, teaching, and resurrection as a counter to the existential void. As Wright observes, on the historical, incarnate premise, Jesus interacts with and meets the human need for abiding meaning and relational responsibility (Wright 1996). Biblical reflection on emptiness thus marks the beginning of an inquiry into the ways Christ offers relational, moral, and eternal significance in a world that sometimes feels devoid of ultimate meaning.

Jesus' Response to the Void

Contemporary nihilism portrays life as fundamentally devoid of significance, questioning whether human labor or achievement can retain enduring meaning. The reflections in the biblical text of Ecclesiastes resonate with this dissonance, concluding that labor, knowledge, or an enjoyable life cannot satisfy the human desire for meaning (Ecclesiastes 1:2). In this context, Jesus enters with a radically different understanding of life, fulfillment, and what it means.

In John 10:10, he states, "I have come that they may have life, and that they may have it more abundantly." This abundance is not something that can be quantified in material wealth, observable success, or according to society's prioritized valuation. It encompasses being in relationships, integrating goodness, and having some awareness of the spiritual. Whereas nihilism reduces existence to cycles of effort with limited enjoyment as consequences, Jesus locates meaning within an experience of integration, relationship, and morality. Living an abundant life is not dependent on what can be verified; it can be seen in our actions, choices, and relationships. However, what it entails is connected to the spiritual, transcendent, and eternal. Søren Kierkegaard's Fear and Trembling reminds us that in the existential engagement with God, it is not so much an abstract concept, but an actual experience, accompanied by passionate engagement (Kierkegaard 1844).

The "life" that Jesus speaks of is not an escape from suffering, social injustice, or the limitations of being human; it brings all of these together as part of a meaningful and relational experience. Nihilism relies on the fundamental premise that meaning must be externally imposed or demonstrably proven, while Jesus grounds meaning in moral obligation, participation, and coherence with God's will. Tillich elaborates that fulfillment emerges from infinite concern, and meaning cannot be disentangled from its relational and transcendent basis (Tillich 1951). In this way, meaning is both intra-referential and

76

relational, situated through others and shaped by ethical discernment.

Relational and moral orientation is at the core of Jesus' mission. Life comes to its full expression through love, commitment to moral action, and attention to others. The nature of his teaching and parables is consistent in locating human action in the relational and beyond self-interest, utility, or time-bound gain. Supporting moral and relational engagement as the primary place of lasting meaning is the command to love God and neighbor (Matthew 22:37-40). Lewis identifies the foundation for human flourishing, as expressed in Mere Christianity, in moral agency and relational goods (Lewis 1952). Knowledge, material accomplishment, or personal achievement cannot account for the depth and coherence of an abundant life. Still, an abundant life fundamentally presupposes ethical action and relational integrity.

An abundant life has an eternal dimension, extending human experience into the purposes of God's kingdom. Jesus locates human existence within a continuum that binds temporal events and significance. Nihilism vacates existence to what's temporal, an isolated existence without regard for enduring meaning; Jesus situates human experience within a moral and spiritual trajectory, where human choices, human relationships, and human character become the foundation of a coherent and lasting purpose. N.T. Wright argues that the historicity of Jesus' life, death, and resurrection demonstrates that meaning is relational and historically grounded, addressing human longing at its roots (Wright 1996).

Throughout this engagement, Jesus reformulates the void holistically. Relational depth, ethical responsibility, and eternal perspective unite and produce a life that is abundant, coherent, and transformative. Where nihilism recognizes the void at its center, he provides significance; where material or empirical metrics do not suffice, Jesus provides value in relational, moral, and spiritual accounts of meaning. This sets up a paradigm for understanding the paradox of the cross, where the sheer incongruence of meaning and apparent defeat becomes the geographical origin of meaning—a dynamic that continues to unfold throughout the Gospels and invites a modern audience to consider it in the midst of profound uncertainty.

The Paradox of the Cross

The cross of Jesus represents a powerful paradox that intersects directly with the challenges of nihilism. It seems at first glance that the crucifixion reinforces the nihilistic perspective of the futility of life. Jesus is crucified, abused, and killed. In the eyes of the world, the act is associated with finality and meaninglessness. The one whose life represented abundance is defeated publicly; the moral and spiritual authority is extinguished. Nihilistic observers would conclude from the cross that even the highest ideals will succumb to impermanence, suffering, and death.

In one sense, the cross parallels the empirical and existential realities of nihilistic considerations. From the perspective of temporality, life is characterized by suffering, injustice, and randomness, a world in which, very often, human effort does not seem to bear any fruit. In the most concentrated expression, the cross embodies the tension surrounding human limitation, the burden of opposition and sin, and the absolute reality of death. Seen purely from the temporal position, the cross confirms the void nihilism laments. Nietzsche, for example, perfectly articulates this sense of human finitude and the "death of God" when he cautions that existence may collapse into despair without some higher grounded significance for the world (Nietzsche 1887).

However, here is where the paradox is found: the resurrection transforms what is final and meaningless into ultimate significance. The act of Jesus's rising does not offer just a symbolic interpretation or a metaphorical lesson; it is framed as a historical occurrence that carries significant moral, relational, and spiritual weight. In Romans 8:18, Paul states, "For I consider that the sufferings of this present time are not worthy to be compared with the glory which shall be revealed in us." Suffering, and what may seem like defeat, are situated within a broader narrative; they are not self-defining, but part of a story that extends beyond empirical evidence and temporal conclusions. Wright reminds us that Jesus' resurrection signifies the intersection of historical reality and divine purpose, where ultimate meaning is simply not found in observable outcomes (Wright 1996).

This paradox challenges the reductive implications of nihilism. Nihilism is right to point to suffering, transience, and human limitation, but cannot account for the transformative reality in which impending defeat is reconstituted to ultimate victory. The resurrection demonstrates that reality is multifaceted, with historical, ethical, relational, and spiritual dimensions intersecting in ways that empirical observation cannot comprehend. John Polkinghorne remarks that such events propose a non-scientific rationale for integrating empirical thought with theology, where meaning is forged not hypothetically, or even programmatically, but as a relational and transcendent reality (Polkinghorne 2004). It can be concluded, therefore, that the cross is an appeal to both limitations of humanity and to transcendence, where the void expressed by nihilism does not disavow its reality.

From the perspective of reflection, the paradox of the cross illustrates a principle central to Jesus' engagement with existential despair. He does not disavow suffering or death, nor does He provide vacuous optimism that denies empirical reality. Rather,

Jesus engages the void and experiences the depth of human limitation, which is then transposed as a new source of meaning and hope through resurrection. Tillich expresses, in a similar form, that 'ultimate concern' responds to the human need for meaning by transmuting despair into a means of engaging reality (Tillich 1951). This relational process provides a template for engaging with nihilism, creating a space for awareness of the void while simultaneously offering a pathway for significance that acknowledges history, ethics, and spiritual ontology.

The cross signifies that ultimate reality does not merely reference the observable or quantifiable. Rather, it is where suffering, morality, relationality, and divine purposes meet in the awareness of suffering. The void of meaning may ultimately not be the endpoint of time, and thus informs a unitary experience that becomes the basis of enduring meaning. The cross is thoroughly paradoxical; it provides both a critique of nihilism and a schema for potential redemption in human history, morality, and experience.

Nihilism, Observation, and Human Insight

Although pessimism is often associated with hopelessness, it remains a valuable perspective from which to examine the human experience. A focus on our fragility and decay—along with the certainty that we will suffer—forces a confrontational approach to our experience, which we are often blind to (or want to be) in more optimistic modes of shaping our experience. After modern technology and empirical understanding have mended our minds to serve us in our daily lives, we must not forget that our lives are still short, the things we create in life are not permanent, and that we cannot know or resolve completely our moral and existential struggles by simply assembling information or relying on rationality. In this way, nihilism helps us understand things—it reveals limitations of humans in the universe, based on empirically grounded observation of human experience that are profoundly important to our existence. What Nietzsche represents as the "death of God" is an awareness of our vulnerability and the fact that we inherit moral systems that don't expose this (Nietzsche 1887).

However, despite the positive aspects of nihilism, it also has numerous limitations. Nihilism has no ethical implications, relational connections, and has no spiritual grounding because all that life represents is ultimately meaningless. It could be said that nihilism articulates both the temporality and fragility of humans, yet gives no account of how to create meaning, act morally, or engage with others in ways that align with the meanings, values, and relationships that provide a deeper meaning in our important spiritual and relational longings. Nihilism is a philosophical approach that involves simply observing and reflecting on the human experience, and it does not fill an existential void. Charles Taylor observes that contemporary secular frames of reference can be coherent in a rationally compelling way (Taylor 2007); however, they often fail to meet the ultimate need for meaning and significance in the human experience.

Jesus, as presented through his life and teachings, offers a rich and integrated understanding of human experience and transcendent reality. Jesus approaches reality with candor. He recognizes suffering, death, and the limits of human possibility, but situates those realities within a deeper, relational, ethical, narrative, and spiritual context. The shortest verse in the Bible, "Jesus wept" (John 11:35), illustrates this. Jesus sees and enters human sorrow, pointing to the seriousness of grief and death. However, in the raising of Lazarus, it is clear that He is claiming these limitations do not exhaust reality as ultimate. There is no denial of the observation of suffering. There is no downplaying of suffering. Instead, it is engaging with life through the registers of ethical relationship and Divine intention (Tillich 1951).

Likewise, in Matthew 6:19-21, Jesus contrasts the accumulation of temporal things with the pursuit of eternal value. He observes that human perception and measurable material success are not sufficient for ultimate fulfillment. He offers a bridge from empirical observation of reality to the transcendent nature of Divine intention for ultimate purpose. Neither observation nor insight is renounced, but both are framed in the relational, moral, and intentional connectedness that clarifies and fosters hope. In similar terms, C.S. Lewis articulates this reality in his book, The Pagan's Progress. It affirms that reality is both observable and morally intelligible, and that human experience is nested within a larger narrative of meaning (Lewis 1952).

From a modern perspective, this approach to achieving integrated meaning and significance poses a challenge to contemporary nihilistic premises. Nihilism can illuminate the void. Nihilism can't bring the possibility of orientation or change. Jesus shows, through both acknowledging the human limits of potential and temporality, as well as being alive to ethics as action, relationship, and spiritual insight, that the emptiness and fragility of things offer no opportunity to prompt ethics, beneficial relationships, and engagement with spiritual insight, even when one is overwhelmed with despair. By engaging with suffering and limits, there is an entry point to an understanding of a reality that is both historical and eternal, empirical and transcendent.

Jesus' approach to constructing meaning through integrated observation and insight validates the awareness of empirical observation while moving meaningfully towards ultimate meaning. Nihilism suggests the fragility and impermanence of life. Even so,

Jesus situates these realities within a coherently observable moral reality and relational significance. Furthermore, human experience, secured in memory, is not lost, nor is it meaningless in losing the observable dimensions of existence that suffering and loss require, if it is made intelligible as part of an observable narrative that includes both the bodily realm and the transcendent quality realm, moving from void to meaning.

Contemporary Cultural Implications

Nihilism's existential concerns are not limited to philosophy and literature; they are also present in contemporary society. Hyper-technological, data-oriented cultures often increase feelings of alienation, anxiety, and meaninglessness. The mental health crises of today, from depression to pervasive existential angst, indicate that material progress or empirical understanding does not create a sense of purpose or meaning. The pace and complexity of modernity, constant access to information, and comparisons of success amplify the sense of precariousness and impermanence. In this way, nihilism may become not the outward display of a theory, but an observable problem for the millions affected by it.

Jesus' framework offers an antidote to this pervasive sense of despair and hopelessness, providing orientation, hope, and relational grounding. He does not dismiss the empirical facts of suffering, impermanence, or human finitude; rather, he provides meaning to these facts through the broader context of moral, spiritual, and relational living. He assures his followers in John 14:27: "Peace I leave with you, My peace I give to you; not as the world gives do I give to you." Here, his peace acknowledges the precariousness and uncertainties of life, providing a foundational sense of peace that transcends time. Abundant life, as stated in John 10:10, is not an

escape from difficulty, but rather a refocusing on what is meaningful through relational and ethical depth gained through experience.

This position carries significant cultural implications today. Empirical observation, technological advancement, and scientific understanding remain important mechanisms in contemporary living; nevertheless, these mechanisms cannot address existential concerns alone. Ethical discernment, relational presence, and spiritual insight work together to situate human behavior within the continuum of significant actions, situated within a broader moral framework. Proverbs 3:5–6 articulates: "Trust in the Lord with all your heart, and lean not on your own understanding; in all your ways acknowledge Him, and He shall direct your paths." The text acknowledges and honors human observation and rational thinking, even as we are reminded that the human aspect of meaning is ultimately framed within the relational and spiritual realm.

Further, Jesus' model also demonstrates that meanings are available even in times of uncertainty. In hyper-technological societies, individuals can become overwhelmed by data, trends, and measurable results, leaving them to struggle to find meaning in what appears to be their own choices, much less in their lives as a whole. Jesus' approach re-contextualizes significance as being relationally grounded, ethically responsible, and spiritually oriented. Both the evidence of experience, observable and the transcendent, can simultaneously exist, and the framework he offers enables all individuals to respond to the complexities of life, rather than resigning to nihilism or despair.

From a cultural perspective, the coexistence of ethical, relational, and spiritual domains alongside observable reality provides a pathway toward resilience, purpose, and ultimately, hope. In this way, it challenges the notion that significance is reducible to something more measurable or to an outcome. It offers an alternative model in which meaning is created through relationships with God, others, and the moral and spiritual order of the world. In this sense, Jesus' framework offers not just comfort, but an orientation to live a life that is abundant, coherent, and indeed ultimately significant, even if one is presently drifting with the flow toward nihilism.

Eternal Significance in a Nihilistic Age

The tension between human frailty and the quest for meaning is still at the center of contemporary experience. In a world of technological acceleration, empirical gauging, and cultural skepticism, many of us live under the weight of transience and uncertainty. Nihilism clarifies the degree of that tension: it reveals the inadequacy of achievement, enjoyment, and knowledge (as an end), but, within the biblical testimony and the life of Jesus, it is not left unresolved. Human observation of finitude and suffering is the lens through which transcendent significance is unveiled.

Jesus' confrontation with the void reframes human fragility as an occasion for relational, moral, and spiritual insight. By dwelling in human suffering and confronting death, there is an affirmation of the reality of limitation; yet, limitation does not characterize ultimate reality. The resurrection redefined apparent finality as enduring significance. Meaning is not an abstraction or temporal success, but lived experience in relational and ethical life. Romans 8:18 captures this dynamic, "For I consider that the sufferings of this present time are not worthy to be compared with the glory which shall be revealed in us."

What follows this frame is a more expansive narrative that locates human life and fragility within the interplay of observation, experience, and ethical reflection. Nihilism rightly identifies the void, indicating what is transitory, fragile, and contingent; yet, the life of Jesus demonstrates that the void is not the end. The void can become the context in which meaning is discovered and engaged, rooted in physical history, moral observance, and relational depth. This perspective challenges current conceptualizations of meaning, necessitating empirical investigation and cultural validation.

In contemporary settings, the realization becomes a concrete reality. Individuals living with uncertainty, alienation, or despair find a model that combines empirical observation, technology, and rational understanding as a means of engagement, situated within a framework that prioritizes relational and ethical meaning. The full life promised in John 10:10 is not a guarantee of physical comfort, but a framework for meaning, purpose, and hope, even when the temporal experience appears devoid of meaning.

In holding the insight of nihilism and the transformative claims of the Gospel, Jesus grounds a radical realism: He neither denies the void nor offers abstract consolation. Meaning emerges relationally, morally, and spiritually, inviting participation in a reality beyond description. Ethical action, historical awareness, and relational connection do not form a layer of existence; they are intimately tied to the work of the void. Life, lived within this context, demonstrates that what looks ephemeral and meaningless can contain significant meaning.

In this sense, human experience can be understood as neither arbitrary nor void. Recognizing fragility and transience creates an opportunity for meaningful relational and ethical discernment, identity, and reflexivity within temporality, and making them covenantally related to a larger, historically and spiritually grounded framework. Jesus' life, death, and resurrection offer an orientation for holding the void: a way of living honorably to what is, but enacting a full narrative of significance.

Nihilism and the Transformative Response of Christ

Nihilism, while uncompromising in its stance, offers a vital perspective on the human condition: its honest views on the limits and fragility of human existence and our eventual mortality (Nietzsche 1887; Taylor 2007). Nihilism draws our attention to the impermanence and apparent futility of our labor, knowledge, and pleasure, while offering a sober clarity about what we often prefer to ignore or dismiss altogether as we encounter parables of empirical observation, cultural optimism, or philosophical distancing from painful realities. Human life, with its unparalleled complexity, is finite; yet achievement or material success does little to alleviate the existential questions that endure across time. In this way, nihilism operates as a diagnostic lens that yields certain truths regarding human vulnerability and the transitory nature of the world in which we live.

The Gospel, however, provides a theological engagement with these truths. Jesus expresses a fullness of the human condition that neither neglects human limits nor denies that suffering and mortality can coexist with an ultimate purpose. The abundant life that Jesus promises in John 10:10 does not suggest temporal comfort or unbroken achievement, but rather a reframing of existence viewed through relational, ethical, and spiritual lenses (Kierkegaard 1843; Barth 1936). Where nihilism portrays a lack, the Gospel discloses a horizon of meaning: Though life is finite, it is enfolded in a meaning-laden reality that is both historical, moral, and transcendent (Wright 1996; Polkinghorne 1989).

This way of thinking makes sense of the empirical, historical, and spiritual dimensions of being human. The observations of impermanence and cycles of suffering and mortality are not denied; rather, they are contextualized within a narrative that invites us to engage relationally, morally, and spiritually, wherever and whenever we may find ourselves. Paul writes in Romans 8:18 that the present sufferings of this time are not worthy to be compared to the glory that is to be revealed. We observe limitations in human existence, and thereby, observation becomes an entry point for understanding the importance of discerning meaning. Recognition of nothingness, or the void, does not eliminate hope; rather, it can lead to flourishing—both ethically and relationally (Lewis 1952; Tillich 1951)—through moral engagement and ethical consideration of our relational context and one another.

The life of Jesus, his death, and his resurrection are the very embodiment of this dynamic. He participates in human suffering completely; he confronts death, experiences seeming defeat, and does not dismiss these realities entirely; rather, these realities are transformed through the resurrection into an enduring meaning. He put into practice a radical realism: the void is not ignored, nor superficially filled; rather, it is thus engaged to be reframed. Meaning emerges within the relational, moral, and spiritual realms, which then orient our meaning-making, enabling action, increasing hope, and extending the meaning-making abilities beyond the observable and measurable (Pascal, 1623; McGrath, 2019).

For contemporary readers navigating despair, alienation, or a sense of meaninglessness, this offers particularly practical clarity. A Gnostic, or non-Gnostic, notion of abundant living may therefore be established; for example, it is not through a sense of knowing, achieving, or mastering technological engagement that an abundant life is achieved. Abundant life is pursued through engaging God relationally, through ethics, and through relationships with others, with God. Once life is recognized as fragile, as it is, that becomes the inquiry into discernment and purpose; and we may then act and participate in the reality where human limitations exist alongside ultimate significance.

Jesus offers a response to nihilism that either denies the reality of human vulnerability or leaves it unaddressed. The Gospel describes impermanence, mortality and apparent futility in terms of ultimately fulfilling purpose, as an abundant and meaning life that is deeply relational, and suffering and the limitations of human existence does not become meaningless, but becomes the very ground in which the empirical, the historical, and the transcendent come together to show that there remains a possibility of lasting significance and hope.

Chapter Six

JESUS AND REALISM: FROM HISTORICAL WITNESS TO MODERN THOUGHT

Foundations of Realism

Realism—here and now—refers to a sense of what is actual, credible, and meaningful. However, the life and message of Jesus suggest one form of realism that knits together the historical, relational, and committed aspects, rather than the reductionist and naturalistic approaches that are popular today. Unlike scientific realism, which restricts knowledge only to events that you can perceive and that observable through experience (Putnam 1975; Bhaskar 1978), and rationalism which tends to posit deduction as its pathway to truth (Descartes 1641; Spinoza 1677),

Jesus' realism recognizes material engagement with the world while embedding social, relational, and ethical meanings in the lived experience. In other words, it is neither abstract nor merely cognitive—it is indeed incarnational. It links the observable reality to moral and relational truth.

The Gospels highlight this evidentiary dimension. "And truly Jesus did many other signs in the presence of His disciples, which are not written in this book; but these are written that you may believe that Jesus is the Christ, the Son of God, and that believing you may have life in His name" (John 20:30–31). The evidence indicated here is not experimental or abstract, as we might recognize science today; it is historical, relational, and ethically significant in meaning. It comes from direct observation of witnesses and reflection of those who experienced Him, offering the reader a concrete link to lived historical existence. The link takes on applied meaning, anticipating critiques of a positivist or reductionist approach, motivated by Charles Taylor's claim in *A Secular Age* (2007) that meaning cannot be constrained to the "immanent frame" nor limited to phenomena observable only by observation or the senses. Human experience, sense of moral obligation, and relational being—which are paramount to the life and message of Jesus—cannot be divorced from truth, and more importantly, the grounding of reality.

By tying meaning to actual, embodied existence, He demonstrates that even in suffering, ethical struggle, or complex human relations, one may retain meaning in life. His life exemplifies how a person can thrive through hardship, as well as in good and meaningful human relations. This kind of realism is rooted in Nietzsche's take on nihilism in *Thus Spoke Zarathustra* (1883), where meaning is voided in the absence of transcendent anchors. Jesus' life—or, in particular, His resurrection—accentuates this tension: He was, in the full sense, a resurrected soul, where suffering and apparent meaninglessness derived significance through the transcendent. By overcoming the forces of death and injustice while revealing meaning through the resurrection point, Jesus' form of realism models how we may integrate historical facts, ethical imperatives, and relational states of being (Barth 1936).

Jesus' realism is historical and existential: it is observably real and ties social and ethical truths, challenges modern reductionist frameworks, and implies that human life is sufficiently framed by lived experience tied to moral obligation, which persists resolutely meaningful. His life and message present a radical, multidimensional framework of realism that has a place and a necessary engagement in contemporary theological, philosophical, and ethical considerations, while remaining anchored in the concrete evidence of lived historical existence.

Jesus and the Modern Mind

For quite a time now, contemporary thought has been inclined toward locating and framing knowledge through evidence that supports rationalism and empiricism (i.e., experience and traditionally held knowledge). Scientific realism grounds knowledge on observation (verification), reproducibility, and measurement, emphasizing empirical aspects of the universe and verifiable aspects of existence (Putnam 1975; Bhaskar 1978). Rationalism prioritizes rational deduction and reasoning for locating truth (Descartes, 1641; Spinoza, 1677), while empiricism locates experience as the fountainhead of knowledge, implying that to some degree, all understanding is directly related to experience through observation of the natural world (Locke, 1690; Hume, 1748). Certainly, these views have experienced tremendous success and generated significant advancements across science, technology, and social organization, shaping modern organizational life in industries, educational institutions, and governments. While both evidence-based and empirical theories introduce explanations for rational or material aspects of reality, often any thought or exploration related to mundane life, thought, or experience invariably overlooks the ethical, relational, and spiritual dimensions of both nature and non-physicality that make sense of human existence. As noted long ago by Alasdair MacIntyre, thought and discourse in modernity tend to degenerate without historical memory and a history of moral tradition (MacIntyre 1981).

Jesus' version of realism aims to incorporate these theories while also transcending their limitations. The life of Jesus, including his miracles and teachings, can be researched historically and associated with a level of locality—relationally—but it also contains infinitely more ethical and spiritual dimensions. John 20:30–31 accounts for the Gospel narratives that serve as testimony, providing evidence of the historical existence of Jesus intended to lead one to believe in and experience life in Him (John 20:30–31). Thus, the truth of Jesus itself is not abstract or intelligible alone; it is relational, ethical, and relates to historical evidence of existence. In contrast to scientific realism, his life relates observation with obligation, responsibility to one another, and moral accountability. In this way, truth is understood as experienced.

This embodied realism also operates in the ethical sphere. His miracles are not only demonstrations of power—they addressed human suffering and relational responsibility, including ethical obligation. The resurrection represents the historical and transcendent distinction: an event that elegantly relates the tension between propositionally verifying the past—that is, the historical aspect—and the transcendent significance. Likewise, his parables, ethical engagement, and achievement in teaching, including the Sermon on the Mount (Matt. 5–7), introduce human experience to

94

ethical and spiritual instruction. His miracles and teachings both embody how lived experience can be transformed and reinterpreted as a means to moral reflection, relational significance, and moral conversation beyond mere relationality.

As N.T. Wright states, "Christian realism…is thoroughly historical, rigorously embodied, and always and everywhere directed beyond itself to God, who has raised Jesus from the dead" (Wright 2003). The life of Jesus teaches us that rationality, moral discernment, and relationality are interdependent and entail shared aspects of perception, meaning, understanding, sight, and mind. His realism challenges us with more than empiricism and evidence-based frameworks; it challenges us with human persons in transition and their obligation to morality and responsibility in relation to one another. The life of Jesus exemplifies the convergence of historical sequence and ethical dimensions, which can be collectively shared among human persons. By integrating historical, ethical, and objectively observed realities with personal epistemology, significance is extended through relational and historical engagement.

The historical events, ethical obligations, and relational realities converge into a holistic frame of truth practice. The life of Jesus provides a paradigm for the modern mind that respects reason, evidence, and observation while simultaneously integrating ethical, relational, and transcendent dimensions that guide human moral frameworks toward meaning beyond the observable.

Pragmatic Implications Today

One can reflect on the historical and moral implications of Jesus' life without being compelled to a theological commitment to it. His life was historically influential in and outside social, cultural, and intellectual contexts, including, but not limited to, his religious commitment. From law, ethics, and literature to art and social justice, Jesus has left a tangible imprint and legacy on civilization. His moral and relational decision-making serves as a real and relatable paradigm for thinking through ethical musings connected to the lived experience of being human. The compassion, justice, and moral discernment of his life create a source of ethos that tensionally connects relational practice to empirical contexts. As the epistle of James states, "faith by itself, if it does not have works, is dead" (James 2:17). This highlights that ethical action and relational responsiveness are integral to how a life is perceived, regardless of a charted theological framework.

Today's reader may be invited into a lived complexity, not merely into an epistemological divide but into an empirical and ethically rational divide. Importantly, in a technological or scientific frame of reference, while we possess a vast number of data points and analytical models, they can provide little more than descriptive narratives, insufficient for prescriptive action. In other words, consider the fields of modern bioethics, artificial intelligence, or medical decision-making, for example; the statistically significant considerations, experimental, or probabilistic readings, can guide a way of understanding what is happening in a complex issue, but do not inherently present justice, human dignity, or relational duty. The life of Jesus serves as a practical example of how observable reality may be connected with ethical reflection. The purpose of these illustrations is to convey that ethics, as a category of human reflection, is far too complex to deduce solely from data and research findings. Ethics requires human interpretation and discernment, and it is about the relationships and responsibilities that we have to respond to one another.

Matthew 25:35 illustrates this: "For I was hungry, and you gave Me food. I was thirsty, and you gave Me drink. I was a stranger, and you took Me in" (Matthew 25:35). What is evident is how ethical action is made more visible and actionable because of relational engagement and spiritual meaning. The actor is expected to care for others regardless of their location within our social structures, and this request underscores the relational nature of ethics and practical ethical reflection. All of the stories of engagement with others that I have cited illustrate, when the actions of Jesus are taken into account, how lived encounters grounded in moral spirit form both the moral reference point and spiritual lens through which we understand and act as humane actors. Ethical responsibilities are not an a priori proposition; they are lived experiences in engagement with real human needs within a socio-historical context.

Even in a post-religious modernity that derives meaning primarily from empirical verification or procedural rationality, the continuing effects of Jesus' life remind us that relational and ethical truths remain a fundamental part of being human. Charles Taylor examines the "immanent frame" in *A Secular Age* (Taylor 2007). He argues that society is dominated by outcomes born from organizations and systems that are increasingly oriented toward measurable or quantifiable reality; however, human flourishing is never solely built on terms of fact or analytical empirical realities. The life of Jesus challenges that uncritical reductionism when he reveals various ethical and relational conditions as vital to what it means to first be human. Compassion, justice, generosity, and moral discernment are not merely philosophical notions—they are enacted social practices that shape culture, social structure, and lived experiences.

Moreover, Jesus' moral influence reaches into the functioning of contemporary civic, social, and even state-supported institutions. Legal systems, philanthropy, education, and human rights initiatives demonstrate how Jesus' life drives ethical and relational engagement and outcomes. The ethical and moral features of Jesus' life are carried forth in secularized forms, underpinning relevant observations on policies and public ethics. Ethical reasoning, relational discernment, and moral courage become the foundations through which human activities are evaluated—not purely for efficiency, but for moral and ethical content. Thus, reflecting on the life of Jesus (historical or secular) as an edifying example offers a practical model to foster actionable ethics in complex modern societies, integrating rational experience evaluation, empirical observation, and moral discernment into action.

The practical implications of Jesus' life today are profound. His historical presence, relational abilities to know one another, and ethical probing all qualify as a lived example worthy of applying to contemporary scenarios. Centering moral engagement where science, technology, and human flourishing intersect becomes a key framework for action. Even in secular or relational contexts, Jesus offers a living model for integrating observation, ethical judgment, and moral action, demonstrating that meaning, purpose, and significance extend beyond empirical data or purely rational frameworks.

Jesus as the Light in the Void

Realism in the life of Jesus delineates the limitations of humanity in ways that bestow transcendent significance. In John's depiction: "In Him was life; and the life was the light of men—and the light shines in darkness, and the darkness did not comprehend it" (John 1:4–5). Where nihilism indicates finitude and emptiness, Jesus represents light—relation, ethics, and transcendence, and light for our humanity that does not fall into futility. This is not only a metaphorical light, but a true relational light that speaks to the human condition. The light corresponds with human limitations, suffering, and disintegration, offering a form of realism that recognizes ethical responsibility, relational awareness, and spiritual awareness as interdependent.

The life of Jesus offers a concrete demonstration of how human beings may encounter existential ambiguity. Nihilism—understood in its various philosophical frameworks—is indicative of meaninglessness, no moral ground or substance to life, effectively, and the fragility of the human attempt (Nietzsche 1883). Yet, through Jesus' relational engagement and ethical living, light emerges within this void. The interaction with the marginalized, compassion, and moral imperatives is a realism rooted in the material yet directed toward transcendent values. It is a form of realism that does not reduce life to only what is empirically real and rational, and accepts that human experience is situated in suffering, relational responsibility, ethical responsibility, and spiritual attunement. In this way, Jesus' light is simultaneously epistemological and practical: it helps illuminate truth or meaningful cognitive knowledge while simultaneously guiding action (Wright 2003).

While scholarship, historiography, and rational inquiry can approach humans as conditions of historical and analytical inquiry, they cannot begin to replicate the lived, expressed experience, ethical, and spiritual expression of the life embodied in Jesus and his life (Crossan 1991; Sanders 1993). It is when we engage with these frameworks alongside the life of Jesus that his "light" moves beyond symbolism to a methodology for navigating human limitations. Historical inquiry can make meaning from events, rational philosophical inquiry can put a structure on meaning-making, and using empirical observations can develop and potentially deepen understandings of meaning. However, no timeline lets us confront the social and temporal conditions of meaning with significance. Jesus' life provides a model to illustrate how human knowledge can cohere with ethical practice, relational commitment, and spiritual purpose (Taylor 2007; MacIntyre 1981).

Moreover, his example serves as a guiding exemplum for navigating the complexities of cultural, technological, and existential fragmentation. In a world dominated by scientific rationalism, digital abstraction, or moral pluralism, human life can often position us toward disengagement, disconnection, loneliness, and ambiguous morality. The realism reflected in the life of Jesus—sometimes recognized as the intersection of historical reality, relational engagement, and transcendent gaze—shows us how to engage. By witnessing the life of Jesus, one can sense a framework, or model, of where historical, relational, and spiritual matters coalesce into meaningful and purposeful living as individuals and the human community (Barth 1936; Wright 1996).

We can observe that Jesus' light shines even in the voids obscured by our nihilism. His life highlights that human existence, with all its finitude, failings, and fragmentation, can still be involved with something transcendent, ethical, and relationally significant. When we engage with the example of Jesus' life, we gain a perspective on our limitations not as deficiencies in meaning, but rather as a moment to be engaged relationally, reflectively, ethically, and, ultimately, spiritually. Jesus' example shows us how to navigate the uncertainties of the contemporary situation with both grounded realism and transcendent hope. His life exemplifies a model for navigating these realities toward human flourishing amidst the complexities and fragmentation of the modern world and the existential doubts that accompany life.

Realism in the Modern Era

Contemporary views prioritize realism in the empirical and rational sense. Scientific realism posits that knowledge must be grounded in what can be observed, replicated, or quantified (Putnam 1975; Bhaskar 1978). Rationalism holds that deductive reasoning, logic, and reason are the principal means of reaching truth (Descartes 1641; Spinoza 1677). Empiricism states that experiential evidence is the source of knowledge (Locke 1690; Hume 1748). Therefore, by combining these views, we have a cosmology in the modern age where what is considered truth tends to be what is demonstrable, verifiable, or logically derived. In this context, qualitative and ethical ideas are often dismissed, relegated to conjecture or mere opinion, due to the modern worldview that prioritizes empirical verification.

While the above views have produced an unprecedented rate of scientific discovery and advancement in social orders, they acknowledge the generous limitation of defining reality narrowly. Human experience has dimensions (ethical, relational, historical, spiritual) that cannot be reduced to observation. The challenge, therefore, is how we understand truth and significance when empirical verification is negated. Yet, most humans will demonstrate a need for truth and significance in their experiences. Alasdair MacIntyre notes this phenomenon in his observation about modern discourse, which tends to fragment when it is delinked from historical and moral traditions (After Virtue, 1981).

Jesus embodies a unique form of realism that meets the expectations of modern thought while still transcending them. In contrast to scientific realism (which is confined to measurable aspects), Jesus' realism is historical and embodied. The Gospels portray Him as a person whose life, teachings, miracles, and resurrection are all observable events with profound ethical and relational implications.

John 20:30-31 highlights the nature of testimony: "And truly Jesus did many other signs in the presence of His disciples, which are not written in this book; but these are written that you may believe that Jesus is the Christ, the Son of God, and that believing you may have life in His name." Here, the realism is grounded not simply in abstract observation, but in relational and historical reality that beckons engagement and discernment.

This is in stark contrast to the abstract ideals often present in philosophical examination. The realism of Jesus is grounded in the flesh-and-blood realities of human existence. It addresses suffering, mortality, and ethical duty, while also avoiding idealism or abstraction. It challenges and anticipates modern nihilism, which interprets the temporality and limits of life as evidence of meaninglessness (Nietzsche, 1862; Camus, 1942). Jesus has shown that meaning rests securely amidst historical, relational, and moral reality, and that life is both empirically observable and ethically and spiritually significant.

This form of introducing realism is especially relevant in an age that favors empirical reasoning. The modern mind demands evidence, and the Gospels position historical testimony, relational encounter, and moral coherence as observable reality. Charles Taylor points out that in modernity, meaning becomes reduced to the "immanent frame." However, religious testimony points beyond narrow reductionism (A Secular Age, 2007). The life of Jesus serves as a bridge between the rigor of empirical observation and the significance of ethical and spiritual depth. This bridge invites the reader to consider a type of truth that is both accessible and transcendent, grounded in history and significant for eternity.

By all means, being considerate of Jesus' realism involves engaging with the strengths of modern thought, while acknowledging its limits. Observation, reason, and empirical analysis all prove essential. Yet, they alone cannot reasonably analyze the relational, ethical, and transcendent aspects of life. Jesus illustrates a realism that transcends measure; the moral, historical, and relational realities of existence signal a life of immeasurable significance and ongoing relevance.

Jesus' Embodied Realism

The contemporary view of realism often favors what can be observed or measured. Scientific realism limits truth to that which can be mathematically or scientifically justified (Putnam 1975; Bhaskar 1978), and rationalism puts deduction and logic as the top priority for certainty (Descartes 1641; Spinoza 1677). But Jesus demonstrates a kind of realism that is neither abstract nor empirical. His truth is relational, historical, and ethical. It is based on flesh-and-blood reality and observable human experience, but is greater than just that which can be measured or computed.

John 20:30-31 addresses the evidential aspects of His life, "And truly Jesus did many other signs in the presence of His disciples, which are not written in this book; but these are written that you may believe that Jesus is the Christ, the Son of God, and that believing you may have life in His name." Again, the focus is testimony, but not the abstract notion of a proposition. The Gospels have a sense of inviting readers into a reality grounded in historical being, where actions, words, and relationships matter morally and spiritually. Importantly, a witness as a focus highlights that truth, while relationally and ethically based, is not arbitrary; it is, in its effect on individuals and communities, accessible, observable, and verifiable.

Jesus' realism is also evident in his own practices. Although there is unmistakable miraculous capability in what Jesus does, he does not perform miracles as simply displays of skill or ability. He intervenes in the pain of human suffering in a last-resort ethical way that engages the relationships between himself and those he encounters. For instance, when providing sight to the blind, feeding those who are hungry, or raising someone from the dead, the miracle acts are grounded in dignity against an immediate felt need that holds both observable engagement and moral consequence. Each miracle encounters human suffering, relational context, and historical circumstance, all illustrating that truth emerges through interaction in addition to abstraction. Similarly, the resurrection of Jesus is offered as a historical reality with implications that extend far beyond the events in time and space. The resurrection shows us that something we might think of as final, like death, defeat, or pain, can be transformed into a lasting significance in history and hold meaning in realities that are morally significant and observable.

In other instances, Jesus teaches through embodied realism, utilizing parables and ethical imperatives that encompass all observable human reality, transforming these indications into moral and spiritual realities. For example, the Sermon on the Mount (Matt. 5-7) provides insights into ethical imperatives from observable life contexts, such as poverty, oppression, and relational conflict, to illustrate a vision of justice, mercy, and relational integrity that transcends these empirical categories. We see in Jesus' teachings both relationally and historically situated language corresponding meaningfully to observables, and the temptation to absolve the practical and historical into something more moral and transformative. Every example demonstrates a form of realist engagement that involves observation in a way that establishes ethical or relational significance.

Compared with the scientific approach of realism, which isolates the phenomenon of observable or measurable things from meaning, or the rationalist camp that abstracts all principles from lived experience, the embodied realism of Jesus demonstrates that truth exists as relational, ethical, and historical engagement. His life offers a model where human observation, moral responsibility, and historical witness meet. Therefore, participation in the world, as Jesus expresses it, while bringing attention to transcending significance, illustrates a model of exploring empirical thought while also expanding the fabric to include moral and relational considerations, in each moment necessary to speak of spiritual realities.

This type of realism presents challenges to contemporary readers in considering the nature of truth. It proposes that the ultimate significance of meaning does not only lie within observable or deduced reasoning, but is found in the history, ethics, and relational presence of others. Therefore, Jesus bridges all the critical elements of empirical reality and transcends to point to a way of thinking about reality that all seek identity and become accessible, deeply subjective, and significantly meaningful. As N. T. Wright explains, "Christian realism is deeply historical, rigorously embodied, and always pointing beyond itself to the God who raised Jesus from the dead" (The Resurrection of the Son of God, 2003).

Jesus and the Response to Nihilism

Nihilism advances to contest the primary presupposition of meaninglessness in life--everyday human contingency, transience, and the futility of seeking, knowing, or enjoying anything. Friedrich Nietzsche famously proclaimed, "God is dead," noting the collapse of transcendent meaning as modernity increased, despite the limitations of his declaration's philosophical meanings (Nietzsche 1974). Martin Heidegger investigated the realm of das Nichts — the nothingness that undergirds and gives shape to conscious existence, highlighting how human awareness confronts an unresolvable emptiness at the center of being (Heidegger 1992). Albert Camus articulated the discovery of the tension between the human quest for meaning and the silence of a universe unconcerned with humanity's significance as "the absurd" (Camus 1991). Solomon summarized the nihilistic challenge eloquently: "Vanity of vanities ... all is vanity." (Eccl. 1:2). While modern frameworks, both rationalist and empirical, can describe limitations in human meaning, they do not address the hunger for meaning that arises when humans confront the emptiness or transience of life. These systems describe "how" and struggle to reach a deeper "why" in the human experience.

Into this void advances Jesus--not as some sort of abstract theoretical idea, but as a real body of flesh and blood. His incarnation illustrates a meaning that is relational, historical, and moral. His life embodied the promise of John 10:10: "I have come that they may have life, and that they may have it more abundantly." Abundant life is not the measure of material things, empirical reasoning, or social position; it fully reveals itself in the relationality of humanity, the morality of being human, and being artfully engaged with being and existence. Human limitation is real; yet, within that limitation lies the possibility of a meaning that transcends empirical studies and abstract theorizing (Kierkegaard 1980).

The crucifixion depicts the engagement vividly. In a sense, it depicts suffering, humiliation, and death--the ultimate things that we think nihilism interprets as meaningless. However, although relationality and morality are currently conceived. The resurrection changes the alleged finality of death into the revelation of meaning as the ultimate purpose--to demonstrate that even the limitations of being human are for enduring meaning, even suffering. Jesus' life then becomes a reality, engaging in what seems like nothing, yet demonstrates a relational ontology of existence that is even more completely consequential of impermanence and uncertainty.

Interaction with Modern Thought

Current thinking about the world is heavily influenced by empiricist and rationalist traditions. Descartes' rationalism centered on clarity, deduction, and what is "self-evident" (Meditations on First Philosophy, 1641), while Hume's empiricism based every aspect of knowledge on direct experience (An Inquiry Concerning Human Understanding, 1748). Later, thinkers such as Karl Popper (The Logic of Scientific Discovery, 1959) and Thomas Kuhn (The Structure of Scientific Revolutions, 1962) contributed to the development and refinement of the "scientific method," which employs observation, measurement, and falsifiability as markers of truth. These perspectives offer invaluable resources for exploring naturalistic phenomena. Still, they have limitations when it comes to questions about relational richness, moral obligation, and ultimate purpose. Everyday experience is often more nuanced than can be measured and/or logically deduced, and it is in that space that Jesus' realism is operational.

The life and teachings of Jesus draw our belief in evidence that is based "below" the modern experience of evidence. John 20:30–3 illustrates the importance of eyewitness testimony as an interlude connecting observable history and relational truth: "And truly Jesus did many other signs in the presence of His disciples, which are not written in this book; but these are written that you may believe that Jesus is the Christ, the Son of God, and that believing you may have life in His name." Here, both the history of the events, the relational interactions, and the moral consequences force us to reckon with the observable human experience, which conveys meaning that cannot be measured or deduced. Evidence is present in observable human experience, but it is embodied, relational, and historically bound; therefore, it cannot be reproduced as an experimental endeavor.

While empirical insight and observation are essential, Jesus leads us to consider these in a way that treats ethics and spirituality as integral to the discernment process. He heals the sick, he feeds the hungry, and he befriends those on the margins of society. All of these activities embody observable qualities, yet they also have relational and moral dimensions. They matter not only in the biological and physical sense but also in the moral and spiritual ones. In this way, what we think of as empirical observation intersects with relational and ethical truth, demonstrating a form of realism that is holistic rather than reductionist.

Reductionist ways of thinking often disconnect phenomena from their ethical, relational, or historical context. Science may produce powerful conclusions for predictions and explanatory descriptions regarding phenomena important in human experience. Still, it risks depersonalizing human beings by treating them as data sets and experiences, rather than as individuals with lived experiences. Similarly, rationalistic systems of thought can abstract principles that limit or engage in an ethical engagement of lived reality. Jesus' realism, instead, situates each moment as part of a broader moral and relational connection. Miracles, parables, and fellowship with disciples display to us that observable reality is inseparable from relational and moral meaning. The world is acknowledged as real, yet human experience is participating in a world that is also ethical, historical, and spiritual.

In engaging modern ways of thinking, Jesus does not dismiss observation, nor does he reject rational thought. He models a synthesis: that what is empirical, what is historical, and what is moral can coalesce in ways that preserve the integrity of observation and also expand the possibilities of meaning. This collective approach also challenges contemporary assumptions that measurable reality is sufficient for meaning. Indeed, Nietzsche reminds us that the collapse of meaning connected to the transcendent can lead us to a state of knowing the facts of life, but then shedding all knowledge as meaningless (The Gay Science, 1882). Jesus, however, does not respond to our attempts to make meaning by denying our facts, but instead integrates them with the relational and moral depth that creates a realism we can orient ourselves with, considering our limitations within its scope as well.

Jesus' situating empirical insights within ethical and relational meaning provides us with a realism that can interact with modern frameworks, but extend beyond their borders. Observation and evidence matter, selected among many forms and variations of knowing to better understand and marvel at the human experience, while simply residing themselves in a wider weave that knits moral responsibility, relational depth, and ultimate significance that cannot be deduced and transposed alone.

Chapter Seven

WHO ARE WE IN HIM?

The Question of Identity in a Modern Context

Contemporary societies often conceptualize human identity using frameworks concerned with the mind, or mind and matter, as matters of observable utility. Rationalism highlights cognitive independence, arguing that what makes our individual selves is our independent reason and ability to determine truth or virtue apart from the authority of others (Descartes, Meditations on First Philosophy, 1641). Empiricism originates from philosophy and focuses on human identity in terms of observable and measurable qualities or traits—such as achievement, skill, and evidence of competence or knowledge (Locke, An Essay Concerning Human Understanding, 1689).

Pragmatism, emerging from various and sometimes contradictory social philosophies and thought, measures human worth or identity in terms of the utility of functional results or a meaningfulness that cannot be disentangled from achieving results (James, Pragmatism, 1907). Nihilism does the opposite, removing the sense of meaningfulness, describing existence as fleeting, empty, or devoid of purpose (Nietzsche, The Gay Science, 1882). Each framework provides a perspective related to the human experience—limitations, the value of knowledge, and the consequences of action—but its own limitations hinder its application of ethical responsibility, ethical human relationships, and the meaningfulness of existence.

Against this background, Jesus offers an alternative framework for defining selfhood. According to Paul, "For whom He foreknew, He also predestined to be conformed to the image of His Son, that He might be the firstborn among many brethren" (Romans 8:29). Here, identity is framed not by criteria that require external judgment or human intellectual achievement, nor for the utility of society, but by an identity gained relationally, with the historical and moral reality exhibited in Christ. The self isn't static or abstract, but develops through engagement with another person who both documents an observable result and contains meaning that transcends the observable result through a life, a teaching, and a pattern of relation. In this sense, identity is both a historical and an ethical event that is developed through an active engagement with a reality that has moral coherence, relational grounding, and historical situatedness.

This paradigm has the capacity to challenge modern philosophies, but it does not reject their contributions. The rationalist's attention to reasoning teaches us about our ability to reflect and discriminate, but it does not account for our relational and moral formation (temporarily attending to Karl Barth, see Church Dogmatics, 1936–

1969). The empiricist and scientistic position acknowledges the importance of measurable evidence; however, it cannot observe the depth of character, relational fidelity, or ethical amendment (temporarily reminding one of Donald Polkinghorne, see Science and Providence, 1989). The pragmatist emphasizes the importance of consequences, but emphasizing utility creates a fragile-willed identity, where there are no lasting relationships (recalling William James' "What Pragmatism Means," 1907). While the nihilist rightly identifies a person's finitude and mortality, it leaves unresolved what to do with the apparent void created by nihilism. (For some reference to Kierkegaard's observation in Fear and Trembling, 1843). The relational and historical identity embodied in Christ describes all the realities above. It situates it within a broader context of moral or spiritual significance, recalling C.S. Lewis in Mere Christianity (1952).

When it comes to identity, does the story of Jesus really reform a person's identity or self? The answer is no in the abstract or idealized sense. However, in the relationship of the person of Jesus Christ, formed in a relationship with the first-century disciples, we will create, consider, and embody the whole of history that is rooted in their present "with them" experience. First-century interaction involves corporeality, the observable, and the relationality of corporeality that continues through Christian contemplation of who they were then "with Him," which is reflected in our contemporary understanding of who we are "in Him" (recalling N.T. Wright, Jesus and the Victory of God, 1996). To be "in Him" is to participate in a reality that is ethical in terms of responsibility, relational in depth, and historical in a situated awareness that allows modern people, living in a techno-empirical-philosophical crisis, to contemplate their self-understanding. There exists substance and coherence that continue to be a focus of understanding ourselves in a technologically conditioned atmosphere of pragmatic identities and moral ambiguity.

Through this lens, identity is a living and dynamic process, and there is no static identity or theoretical concept for it. A person's human activity can have integrity (including the fragility of being human, as well as the success and failure of being human) within a moral, relational, and historical situatedness, creating a coherent understanding of "who we are in Him." This understanding is a position, not just an attribute.

Identity as Relational and Historical Reality

In the context of Jesus' life and teachings, human identity is not merely a philosophical ideal or theoretical construct. It is embodied, observable, and ethically significant, lived out in relational engagement and ethical practice. The biblical understanding of identity is radically different from philosophies that reduce identity to cognition, measurable characteristics, or functional outcomes. The biblical understanding of the self is situated in actual historical reality and relational participation, with identity formation emerging through engagement with Christ and his teachings (Barth, Church Dogmatics, 1936-1969; Lewis, Mere Christianity, 1952).

Paul's writings illustrate this relational understanding of identity. In 2 Corinthians 3:18, he notes, "But we all, with unveiled face, beholding as in a mirror the glory of the Lord, are being transformed into the same image from glory to glory, just as by the Spirit of the Lord." Transformation is a relational, ongoing, and historical process. Identity develops over time through participation in the lived experience of the moral and relational framework provided by Christ. Identity formation is not based on immediate knowledge or theoretical awareness. Identity is formed through a firsthand account of historical reality and observable practices, including decision-making, relational engagement, and ethical choices that signify alignment with a historical figure who provides a moral and ethical framework (Wright, Jesus and the Victory of God, 1996).

Identity is also rooted in relational participation, as noted in John 15:4-5, "Abide in Me, and I in you."As the branch cannot bear fruit of itself unless it abides in the vine, neither can you, unless you abide in Me. I am the vine, you are the branches. He who abides in Me, and I in him, bears much fruit; for without Me you can do nothing." Identity is related and sustained by connection to Christ, producing observable results, or "fruit," that demonstrate ethical behavior, moral discernment, and relational integrity. This relational reality starkly contrasts rationalist approaches, which may treat the self simply as a rational agent, or observational approaches, which may measure only the measurable properties or indicators of identity socially (Kierkegaard, Fear and Trembling, 1843; Locke, An Essay Concerning Human Understanding, 1689). In both cases, the moral dimension is at risk of being minimized or surpassed.

When identity is established in relational and historical realities, it helps to frame the moral and existential limits of modern philosophies. Rationalism implies an independence of thought, but it may abstract ethical consequences from the thought process. Empiricism prioritizes the observable, but it cannot account for moral change or the depth of relationships. Pragmatism assesses worth by outcomes, but outcomes alone, without a relationship and moral context, cannot account for identity (James, Pragmatism, 1907).

Nihilism acknowledges human limits and mortality, but doesn't resolve the empty existential void (Nietzsche, The Gay Science, 1882). Identity in Christ acknowledges these insights while providing an identity framework that transcends reductionism, accounting for both observable and meaningful relational and moral histories (Polkinghorne, Science and Providence, 1989).

In practical terms, this relational and historical identity can be demonstrated through human actions and societal involvement, as well as in how we link morals, ethics, and decision-making to one of the three modes of existence. Relationships and historical realities are reflected in how we respond to moral dilemmas, cultivate relationships, and serve our community, demonstrating a likeness to the moral and relational patterns established by Jesus. These dimensions are measurable in their effects, but they derive their meaning from the historical spirit and reality, as human identity is both situated and transcendent (Lewis, 1952; Wright, 1996).

Therefore, identity as relational and historical reality offers a robust framework for rationalizing selfhood in the modern age. It connects intellectual, moral, and historical realities, providing coherence, a framework, and a mode of understanding human experience— achievements, failures, and limits —in the light of relationships and moral truth. This perspective prepares the reader to engage with and address relational and moral questions that arise from the interaction of a Christ-centered identity with rationalism, empiricism, pragmatism, and nihilism in a chronological context.

Engaging Modern Philosophies

Recognizing identity in Christ as both relational and historically situated entails examining how this perspective of self compares to the dominant modern philosophies. Each worldview—rationalism, empiricism, pragmatism, and nihilism—has the potential to describe aspects of human experience, yet each also has fundamental limitations when it comes to understanding the full complexity of

116

identity. The life and teachings of Jesus offer a model that addresses the merits of each, while asserting a transcendent model that draws from moral, relational, and historical dimensions (Kierkegaard, Fear and Trembling, 1843; Barth, Church Dogmatics, 1936-1969).

Rationalism emphasizes the autonomy of thought and the supremacy of reason in defining our knowledge of ourselves. Contemporary rationalist models often imply that one's reasoning is enough to define identity, ethics, and purpose. At the same time, intellectual reflection may remove the self from a historical and relational context. A biblically grounded conception of the self locates identity in relational participation with Christ. Romans 8:29 clarifies that the self is not solely defined by autonomous thought, but rather a self that is aligned—involved—with the historically real and morally grounded life of Jesus. We appreciate thought and reflection, yet identity remains incomplete without relational and ethical context (Tillich, Systematic Theology, 1951; Taylor, A Secular Age, 2007).

Empiricism and scientism, in contrast, claim observables and measurable phenomena to ground reality. Within these models, identity may be reduced to observable traits, outcomes, or behaviors. Although empirical observation relies on pattern recognition and human potential, it is inherently incapable of constructing the moral and relational formation needed to provide a full account of identity. The embodied realism of Jesus reveals the limits of empirical observation: to observe the teachings, miracles, and experiences of Jesus is to witness their effects; yet, the implications of His life cannot be reduced to observational experience. Therefore, John 15:4–5 articulates abiding textually in relation to the significance of "fruit," which follows the connection with and to Jesus. The observable—"fruit"—follows from the establishment and sustenance of the relationship with Jesus, but it is not an observable feature (Polkinghorne, Science and Providence, 1989; McGrath, Science & Religion, 2010).

Pragmatism evaluates identity based on utility and effectiveness, and all significance pertains to results or consequences of action. While pragmatism is correct in acknowledging that human choice produces observable outcomes, it can overlook the relational or ethical processes through which choice may yield these outcomes. A Christ-focused view of identity demonstrates that moral and relational formation are necessary foundations for generating meaning and making action significant. By operating within ethical and historical patterns established by Jesus, the believer's effectiveness is grounded in both accomplished observable impact and fidelity to moral and relational integrity (James, Pragmatism, 1907; Smith, How (Not) to Be Secular, 2014).

Nihilism argues against the existence of inherent meaning, representing human existence as void or temporary, rather than fixed or enduring. While nihilism accurately conveys the conditions of mortality, fragility, and limitation, nihilism argues against the system of reference for significance or the relational ground for meaning itself. Jesus enters this frame directly by representing identity as firmly situated in a historically and morally situated reality. The cross and resurrection mark a plain voidness and defeat. Yet, they reconcile for ultimate significance, offering a form of identity that is relational, historical, and morally coherent (Nietzsche, The Gay Science, 1882; Wright, Jesus and the Victory of God, 1996).

Together, these frames trace the contours of human self-understanding, yet each perspective loses value in consideration of the whole. Jesus's comportment integrates the respective insight while advancing beyond limitation. Reason, observable emphasis, practical action, and awareness of the human condition in a world marked by terror or fragility are aspects of His unique and counter-narrative understanding in the establishment of selfhood formed within the limited experience of modernity. Thus, he offers a model of human selfhood intelligible to modern thought and yet saturated in the discourse frame of a biblical narrative. This legacy offers a writer's lens for evaluating the intersecting nuances of intellect, observation, utility, and existential prompts for the twenty-first-century reader (Lewis, Mere Christianity, 1952; Aquinas, Summa Theologica, 1274).

Living as His Children: Ethical and Relational Implications

Identity in Christ is much more than a philosophical/logical thought experiment; identity is ethical, relational, and performed. The idea of being "children of God" has ethical implications: human actions, decisions, and interactions can be observable manifestations of living in and in accordance with Christ's ethical and relational reality. This means that identity can be understood in historical and relational-practical terms rather than as an abstract idea (Kierkegaard, Fear and Trembling, 1843; Barth, Church Dogmatics, 1936-1969).

An ethical responsibility is at the center. To be His children is to act in terms of grace, humility, and truth in decision-making and social action/work. Grace orders action so that humans can act with patience, forgiveness, and sensitivity to the relational aspects of choice. Humility situates a person as a historical, relational being, with limits encountered and situated in reference to a more significant moral framework. Truth operates as a standard/guideline offering moral discernment and relational integrity. These are not abstract ideals; they are observable, and one can witness them in the choices made in personal relationships, professional endeavors, or civic engagement. In a world that increasingly favors appeals to empiricism, technology, and reductionist reasoning, the ethical-relational domain subverts/enters a coherent, grounded identity in a world characterized by instrumental or outcome-based definitions of selfhood (Lewis, Mere Christianity, 1952; McGrath, Science & Religion, 2010). Galatians 2:20 demonstrates the concrete, lived reality of this identity: "I have been crucified with Christ; it is no longer I who live, but Christ lives in me; and the life I now live in the flesh I live by faith in the Son of God, who loved me and gave himself for me." Here, Paul's identity is presented as an ongoing, observable transformation—an expression of Christ's moral and relational reality, as it is lived out in human action. Therefore, ethical conduct, relational engagement, and moral discernment are both measurable and transcendent, providing evidence of the relational, historical, and moral nature of selfhood in Christ (Tillich, Systematic Theology, 1951; Wright, Jesus and the Victory of God, 1996).

This framework is also in meaningful dialogue with modern philosophies. The emphasis of rationalism upon autonomous reason becomes especially clear when it is moral responsibility and relational integrity that deliver meaning to intellectual application. When it comes to Empiricism and scientism, they acknowledge observable consequences. Identity in Christ is what makes all the difference, in that it finds those consequences anchored in moral and relational significance. Pragmatism values actionable efficiency. The ethical formation of the individual, however, ensures that behavior leads to consequential outcomes rooted in a relational and moral reality. Nihilism emphasizes human limitations. Relational and ethical identity in Christ locates those limitations within the factor of purpose, historical significance, and moral accountability (Taylor, A Secular Age, 2007; Smith, How (Not) to Be Secular, 2014).

Practically speaking, to live actively as His children requires observable behaviors. How one responds to conflict, enters community, makes decisions under uncertainty, builds relationships, or exerts influence in social or professional ways. Identity is observable through action, while behaviors cannot be separated from relational and moral formation; they connect the empirical, historical, and ethical experience of individuals. By bringing these together, identity centered in Christ provides an experience of an identity grounded in ongoing action and behavior, as a means through which we navigate contemporary challenges and avoid mischaracterizing human selfhood as mere utility, data, or a product of existential necessity (Polkinghorne, Science and Providence, 1989; McGrath, The Big Question, 2001).

Ultimately, living as His children reflects an actually coherent, actionable, and morally grounded identity that is relationally sustained, historically contingent, ethically informed, and practically observable—a selfhood that demonstrates the abiding significance of Jesus' life and teaching in the twenty-first century. Consequently, identity becomes a perspective of engagement—shaping behavior, facilitating decision-making, and informing action in social contexts—while taking a meaningful shape that is observably significant and morally grounded in the realities of modern life.

Identity in Dialogue with Contemporary Thought

In the twenty-first century, technology, culture, and society continually shape and influence identity and the formation of identity, while simultaneously creating new challenges to the concept of identity. Personal and social value often assumes a quantitative measure in the modern world: social media impressions (and likes), professional performance metrics and indicators, and performance metrics for evaluating success represent social assessments of value. Public narratives create leverage for quantifying stories and value in these areas by encapsulating achievement in an idea of progress, whether in terms of efficiency or visibility. Thus, we may face a scenario in which identity is narrowed into quantifiable measuring outputs—i.e., pattern or representative metrics that often fail to capture the relational, ethical, and historical relevance of one's identity (Taylor, A Secular Age, 2007; Smith, How (Not) to Be Secular, 2014).

Jesus' embodied realism provides a way to navigate identity and identity challenges without resorting to reductionistic views of identity. Jesus' life, moral, and ethical teachings invite us into a baptismal existence derived from a relational and historical standpoint, and that morality and ethics are not distinguishable but arise as insights arrived at through observably ethical action. Values gained from rational reasoning, objective empirical observation, and social analysis bring forth an epistemology of understanding the inner workings of humans and the worlds in which we are a part, with the capacity to observe patterns, clarify consequences, and exhibit social will (and reason) to navigate human behavior. Yet, as insightful and constructive as these frameworks may be, they cannot account for the fullness of what it means to define oneself. Identity is more than what can be measured, or observed, or instrumentally functional—identity must also include relational depth, moral insight, and participation in a historic space of living into existence derived from the life of Christ and his teaching (Kierkegaard, Fear and Trembling, 1843; Barth, Church Dogmatics, 1936–1969).

Moral insight and relational insight interact with observable reality to cohere identity beyond quantifiable results. Galatians 2:20 describes this reality, where living in Christ signifies moral truth and relational actions that can be observed in daily choices, societal relationships, and public social responsibilities. Thus, ultimately, identity (self) is both pragmatic and transcendent. Pragmatic in the way self appears through ethical interaction and behavior in society, and transcendent in the way that ethical behaviors reflect assent to a historic and moral coherence from a significantly relational framework with Christ and his teaching, that is not reducible to quantifiable outcomes or instrumentally functional perspectives (Tillich, Systematic Theology, 1951; Lewis, Mere Christianity, 1952).

Pressures in culture and society today often underscore improvement, development, productivity, visibility, or comparative advantage, often with the unspoken implication that worth or value is determined by one's performance or modifiable change. In contrast, the identity formed in Jesus suggests a different narrative: worth does not lie in results but rather in relational integrity, moral accountability, and agency within the world. Rather than diminishing worth, human finitude is taken up into purposefulness in the historical continuity of Jesus' life and redemptive work. This enables my professional, social, or personal decision-making to be informed by moral conviction and relational awareness, being informed but not limited by empirical judgment, allowing for originality while resisting the expectations of purely abstract and empirical measures of worth and identity (Polkinghorne, 1989; McGrath, 2001).

In contemporary thought, navigating identity through a model of identity in Christ is a lens towards coherence and resilience. It allows room for the limits of humanity, acknowledges the realities of the social world and social/cultural technologies, exercises reason informed by empirical insights, while concurrently situating the self in a grounded and historically coherent space that is relational, ethically situated, and historically situated. Thus the lens, and model of identity in Christ allows engagement with contemporary pressures and challenges (digital, culture, and societal) in a manner that is systemic and does not resort to reductionism; potentially offering a space of coherency, purpose, and space of stability in spaces of multiple references to enduring significance (Wright, Jesus and the Victory of God, 1996; McGrath, Science & Religion, 2010).

Forward Transition

The previous argument has established that identity in Christ is neither a conception nor a collection of idealized virtues. Rather, it is historical, relational, ethical, and transcendent, arising from engagement with the life, teaching, and moral reality of Jesus, expressed in observable, demonstrable ways, and grounded in a framework that accounts for moral formation, relational engagement, and historical awareness. It is not merely internalized beliefs or morally aspirational traits—it is a lived reality, embodied in how people act, make decisions, and engage in relational and social structures. In this sense, the Gospel presents Jesus not as a remote ideal, but as a historical and relational presence that continues to shape the human experience in the present (Barth, Church Dogmatics, 1936–1969; Wright, Jesus and the Victory of God, 1996).

Identity in Christ also dynamically interacts with the contemporary intellectual context. Rationalism emphasizes the autonomy of thought and the rational evaluation of historical knowledge, as well as critical reasoning and logical relationships. Empiricism and Scientism emphasize observation, observable phenomena, and measurable data. Pragmatism emphasizes outcome and effectiveness. Nihilism emphasizes mortality, transience, and the potential meaninglessness of human existence. Each offers insight into the human condition and obstacles to living meaningfully in the complexity of contemporary existence. Each also highlights the limits of the perspective when considered alone. Rationalism, for example, is useful yet has the potential to abstract from the relational and moral (Kierkegaard, Fear and Trembling, 1843). While empiricism and scientism clarify aspects of the patterns of reality, they are unable to account for ultimate purpose, ethical formation, or relational depth. Pragmatism stresses outcomes but may ignore the processes of character and moral development. Nihilism speaks to human fragility and limitation while asking questions related to existence.

Jesus' life and teaching offer a framework for engaging with each of these insights, while surpassing their limits. While affirming reason, observation, and practical outcomes, Jesus organizes these insights within a relational and historical reality that possesses ethical coherence. Romans 8:29 frames the believer's transformation in relational terms: "For whom He foreknew, He also predestined to be conformed to the image of His Son." Thus, identity is a process, not solely determined by abstraction, empiricism, or instrumental effectiveness, but shaped by participation in an ethically and relationally oriented reality that is grounded in history. Galatians 2:20 speaks helpfully of the practical and embodied nature of this identity: "I have been crucified with Christ; it is no longer I who live, but Christ lives in me; and the life which I now live in the flesh I live by faith in the Son of God, who loved me and gave Himself for me." Moral discernment, ethical action, and relational participation are the observable outcomes of living from the reality of Christ.

This framework provides a bridge between observation and meaning, intellect and ethics, empirical reality and moral orientation. Being in Christ is not a passing, detached, or disengaged stance from modern existence and the centuries of technological, cultural, and social pressures that surround it, but rather forms a basis for navigating such experiences and resisting reductionism. It combines empirical insights, rational reflection, and pragmatism with relation and ethical coherence. In this way, identity can be understood as simultaneously intelligible to modern analytical frameworks and deeply rooted in a historical, moral, and relational reality.

The forward motion of the discussion could not be more precise. Having cleared the space for identity in Christ with respect to the relational, historical, and ethical dimensions of identity, we now turn to the practical application. How does this framework make for engagement in everyday decision-making, social action, moral decision-making, and responding to existential questions? How does it create coherence for living in a world formed from data, uncertainty, and fast-paced technological changes? The next chapters will address these questions, demonstrating how identity, meaning, and moral responsibility are lived realities—observable, actionable, persistent—existing in the ongoing influence of Jesus the historical and moral agent.

In this way, the argument shifts smoothly from conceptual inquiry to practical engagement, demonstrating that identity in Christ is not a conceptual ideal, but a lived, historically situated, ethically integrated, and relationally involved reality that engages with modern thought and existence (Wright; Taylor).

Chapter Eight

LIVING REALISTICALLY IN CHRIST: IDENTITY, MEANING, AND ACTION

*I*n the contemporary world, we live in an increasingly technological and data-rich era, alongside philosophical challenges to rationalism, empiricism, pragmatism, scientism, and nihilism. In these paradigms, humanity seeks understanding, purpose, and meaning of self. Each perspective offers an exploration of our human condition. Still, it will encounter limits when dealing with life's full complexity, meaning, and relational existence. Rationalism can explain logical consistency, but it may overlook relational and moral coherence (Aquinas, 1225-1274; Taylor, 2007). Empiricism presents explicable concepts of the observable and measurable, but it cannot provide ultimate purpose (McGrath 2010; Polkinghorne 1989). Pragmatism empowers one's practical use of their own meaning but may fail to recognize formative processes (Smith 2014). Nihilism reveals human fallibility, but it leaves the question of meaning with no answer (Pascal 1623-1662; Kierkegaard 1813-1855). Scientism excels in explaining natural order, but it struggles in the realms of morality and spirituality (Craig 2008).

In the context of Christianity, the life, teaching, miracles, and resurrection of Jesus provide a platform that engages these modern lenses without minimizing or dismissing them. He proposes a historically substantiated, relationally anchored, and ethically consistent reality, where identity, meaning, and moral actions are intertwined. An example of a relational dimension is expressed in Romans 8:29: "For whom He foreknew, He also predestined to be conformed to the image of His Son". For an example of the practical, lived dimension, consider Galatians 2:20: "It is no longer I who live, but Christ lives in me." Identity in Christ has both observable and transcendent aspects: ethical discernment, relational engagement, and historical grounding (Wright 1996; Sanders 1993; Crossan 1991).

This combination enables a response to twenty-first-century challenges without resorting to reductionism. Technology, social constructs, and empirical evidence are engaged with, yet through the lens of relational, ethical, and historical reality (Lewis, 1952; McGrath, 2010). Human actions, decisions, and participation in society become the means by which a self acquires relational, ethical, and historical qualities. The model demonstrates that significance, purpose, and identity have not simply disappeared into a world of data, skepticism, or indifference, but rather weave together an engagement of intellect, observation, utility, and relational depth (Polkinghorne 1989; Tillich 1951–1963).

Furthermore, the life of Jesus provides a lens for addressing suffering, ambiguity, and limitation. The cross and resurrection demonstrate how a clear triumph over apparent defeat, and the lack of existential meaning, can be transformed into ultimate meaning, thereby coping with nihilism and the limitations of empiricism and rationalism that venture into pure reductionism (Kierkegaard 1843/1985; Barth 1936–1969). Meaning, relational depth, and moral coherence come not from abstraction, but from real historical lived experience aligned relationally and ethically with Christ (Taylor 2007; Smith 2014).

In conclusion, the book invites readers into a reality in which identity, meaning, and action continually reinforce and contribute to responses. The significant intersection of rational thought and empirical observation, along with practical reasoning and ethical reflection, occurs within the historical, relational, and moral reality of Jesus' life. Modern philosophies offer helpful tools for understanding the human experience, while a Christ-centered realism provides a meaningful and coherent integration of approaches to moral reasoning, alongside empirical thinking (Lewis, 1952; Wright, 1996; Craig, 2008).

In a world that has grown increasingly skeptical, technology-laden, and measurement-driven, living life realistically in Christ means engaging with your intellect, observation, and practicality without losing sight of moral and relational truth. Identity is historical, relational, and ethical; meaning is relationally and ethically coherent; and action is coherently led by integrity and fidelity in relationship. This is not an invitation to undefined abstraction, but a demonstration of living life in Christ as a reality, waiting, observing, ethically grounded, relationally robust, and historically significant (Aquinas 1225–1274; Pascal 1623–1662; Polkinghorne 1989).

By reestablishing Jesus as a radical realist, this chapter has shown that His life speaks into the twenty-first century just as powerfully as it did in destabilizing assumptions two thousand years ago. Humans can live with coherence, purpose, and relational integrity within a world that has been shaped by science, technology, and skepticism, without giving up the depth of meaning and ethical weight of what it means to live a genuine human life (Barth 1936–1969; Tillich 1951–1963; McGrath 2010).

Bridging Worldviews and Reality

The landscape of the twenty-first century is one in which rapid technological development, data-informed decision-making, and all-encompassing skepticism dominate. Multiple frames of thought shape human thinking, including rationalism, empiricism, pragmatism, scientism, and nihilism. While each offers a valuable perspective on the structures, processes, and limits of human beings, each also masks an important insight into the human condition. Rationalism emphasizes logic, coherence, and the dignity of reason; however, it remains vulnerable to detachment from the relational and moral dimensions of existence (Aquinas 1225-1274; Taylor 2007). Empiricism and scientism emphasize observation, measurable phenomena, and empirical verification; yet, they cannot attend to ultimate purpose, ethical responsibility, or the richness of human experience (McGrath 2010; Polkinghorne 1989). Pragmatism judges truth and utility based on outcomes, which often reduces moral and relational nuance to efficiency (Smith 2014); whereas nihilism uncovers human fragility, mortality, and the possibility of life's meaninglessness (Pascal 1623-1662; Kierkegaard 1843/1985; Craig 2008).

Each of these frames, unpacked individually, offers insight into the human condition, highlighting patterns, causal relationships, and practical implications. They cause us to sharpen our analytical skills, offer us tools to think about what we observe in natural and social processes, and invite us to ask questions about human limitations (Lewis 1952; Wright 1996). However, each cannot stand alone without significant limitations. For example, rationalism fails to resolve moral purpose (Aquinas 1225-1274). Even at its most rigorous, empiricism cannot measure relational depth or ethical integrity (McGrath 2010). Lastly, pragmatism risks flattening existence into short-term utility (Smith 2014). Nihilism cautions us of mortality and contingency while simultaneously often refusing to offer any grounding for hope, meaning, and relational fidelity (Kierkegaard 1843/1985; Pascal 1623–1662). Together, they present a world that is simultaneously aware of complexity and restriction— but also vulnerable to reductionism, despair, and a disconnection from the self.

Into this, enters Jesus as a historically located, relationally active, and ethically coherent presence, who neither dismisses the insights of reason, observation, or practical consequence, nor allows them to constitute the totality of human comprehension. Instead, He critically and creatively engages these tensions to convey that truth, meaning, and identity cannot be separated from relational, historical, and moral realities. John 1:14 presents the incarnation as the ultimate reference point for grounded reality: "The Word became flesh and dwelt among us, and we beheld His glory, the glory as of the only begotten of the Father, full of grace and truth." Jesus' life— his interactions, teachings, miracles, and resurrection—provides a rationale for accounting for the human being that does not abstract the human being from life, while also not reducing life to observable measures (Barth 1936-1969; Tillich 1951-1963; Wright 1996).

In relation to rationalism, Jesus exemplifies a supra-rational wisdom: his parables invite reconsideration of normative logic, exposing contradictions and assumptions, while also offering ethical clarity and relational insight (Luke 10:25-37; Kierkegaard 1843/1985). In relation to empiricism and scientism, he acknowledges observation and evidence—invites Thomas to touch his wounds—but at the same time, asserts that faith and historical witness reach beyond the limits of what can be seen and established by sensory verification (John 20:24-29; Polkinghorne 1989). Pragmatism is engaged through practical action: healing, feeding, teaching, and serving. Yet, true value is not measured by immediate utility, but rather by lasting ethical and relational outcomes (Luke 9:23; Lewis, 1952). Nihilism is also addressed through the reality of the cross and resurrection; what seems like defeat and meaninglessness becomes the context of ultimate meaning, offering relational and historical qualifiers for human identity and purpose (John 10:10; Ecclesiastes 1:2; Pascal, 1623-1662).

Jesus then functions as an integrating figure, synthesizing the insights gained from multiple worldviews and understanding the limitations that exist in each. Identity, meaning, and moral action are not left fragmented between observation and logic, and utility and despair, but coherently situated within historic, relational, and ethical reality. The invitation for readers becomes one of exploring a framework that is not only intellectually rigorous and morally coherent in its intellectual justification, but also empirically aware and relationally grounded in practical action, and the past is ethically qualified (Sanders, 1993; Crossan, 1991; McGrath, 2010).

This chapter begins to explore the notion of identity, meaning, and action, where these constructs are seen as being incorporated into Christ's reality. The discussion moves from conceptual synthesis to practical synthesis for living in a world that is complex technologically, tentative morally, and uncertain existentially. Framing the discussion in this way means that acknowledging the 'space' of insights gained from modern thinking does not mean rejecting or failing to acknowledge modern thinking. Rather, it draws modern thinking into a space of living that is configured by historical reality, relational fidelity, and ethical coherence, which set boundaries for human life (Taylor 2007; Smith 2014).

Historical and Relational Reality of Christ

The main idea in this volume is that Jesus is not a vague abstraction, not simply a symbol, but a concrete presence whose life, teachings, and activities were rooted in an actual historical context that continues to guide human thought and action. The important words of John 1:14 relate, "The Word became flesh and dwelt among us, and we beheld His glory, the glory as of the only begotten of the Father, full of grace and truth." This is not just theological rhetoric; it connects identity, meaning, and relational reality with the specific experience of existence as it is engaged in history. The Gospels affirm the embodied life of Jesus through the repeated accounts of His hunger, tiredness, conversation, and suffering in the text. He is undoubtedly a person alive and present, historically located in a particular time and place, visible and verifiable, not an abstract spectator hovering above our quotidian life (Barth 1936-1969; Wright 1996).

The author reinforces the historical dimension in John 20:30-3, when he recorded: "And truly Jesus did many other signs in the presence of His disciples, which are not written in this book; but these are written that you may believe that Jesus is the Christ, the Son of God and that believing you may have life in His name." The author makes an explicit connection between eyewitness accounts of Jesus, resulting in relational and moral action. The miracles, connections, and teachings of Jesus are not just demonstrations of the supernatural; they are relational actions that shape our moral and historical lives. The observation of Jesus' actions provides support for a coherent ethical reality in which relational and moral significance cannot be separated from historical fact.

This historic reality is deeply interconnected with relational significance. Jesus' teachings were not abstracted in philosophical treatises; they were part of contextual human experiences—food, travel, commerce, and human-to-human exchanges. Parables were not mere intellectual endeavors; they were relational invitations that invited the listener to reconsider their moral assumptions of relational priority. Jesus' engagement with the disenfranchised, sick, and ostracized exemplifies that historical presence sustains ethical energy. Thus, observing Jesus' life and engaging with it provides a model for discerning moral and relational reality, and brings into question whether identity and meaning are found in abstractions, but rather in lived, relationally embodied expectations (Kierkegaard 1843/1985; Lewis 1952).

The resurrection adds an ethical-transcendent dimension of interweaving with historical fact. Rather than allegorical, the New Testament portrays the resurrection as an event confirmed by history, carrying tremendous ethical and relational significance. The behavior of the disciples and the early Christian communities, along with the historical witness that followed, confirm that the moral and relational dimensions of Jesus' life cannot be separated from the historical reality of that life. Historical and ethical events, such as timed and ethically implemented miracles, death, and resurrection, participate in a sustained, ongoing presence in history. The miracles, death, and resurrection are witnesses to a reality that brings time and eternity together, and as such, also resist scientific reductionism, nihilism, and narrowly pragmatic reasoning (Crossan 1991; McGrath 2010).

Therefore, to understand Jesus in the light of these historical and resourceful constraints shifts the conversation regarding considerations of identity, meaning, and purpose from abstract ideas or measures to a relational, historical, and resourceful true reality. Thus, for real faith is neither irrational nor detached from lived and observed existence, but tethered to historical events enacted with relational reality. Ethical consideration, moral discernment, and relational engagement should be informed by the life of a true historical figure who exemplified principles that embody or display what it means to live ethically, thereby cohering relational concepts (Barth 1936-1969; Wright 1996).

In modern times, this line of thinking and action has real consequences. In a world dominated by data-driven thinking, technological efficiency, and reductionist reasoning, seeing the Jesus experience through historical relational reality offers a framework for understanding what it means to engage with identity, purpose, and ethical relational action. Human existence cannot be reduced to engendered patterns or instrumental success; human existence is conditioned or resourced in the relational-historical reality of coherence, which aids direction and moral constraint. By considering Jesus as an experienced and engaging historical relational figure, this attempt seeks to establish a bridge between modern-day, framed intellectual reasoning and the lived experiences of moral and relational realities (Taylor 2007; Smith 2014).

Thus, a historical relational reality of Christ is the anchoring of a coherent identity and ethical discernment, or relational correctness, which provides an equally framed lens for modern-day thought, observation, and practical reasoning to cohere and engage, rather than simply reducing to two conceptual ideas or frames. Ties to observing and engaging with places humans in these issues of historical-relational moral and relational significance or value, while standing in a prepared mode to encounter modern issues framed by tenets of insight and coherence, with altitudes of ethical significance.

Integrating Modern Philosophies

Contemporary existence is shaped by various systems of thought that aim to elucidate reality and the human condition, including rationalism, empiricism, pragmatism, scientism, and nihilism. All of these styles of thought reveal facets of reality; however, none fully expresses the profundity of identity, meaning, and ethical obligation. The life and teachings of Jesus offer avenues for engaging with, critiquing, and synthesizing these systems of thought, providing a coherent approach to understanding what is observable, what is reasoned, what is consequential, and what is meaningfully defined (Lewis 1952; Wright 1996).

Rationalism prioritizes logic, coherence, and systematic logic. Rationalism seeks to define what is true through deduction and a line of consistent reasoning, on the basis that the human intellect can arrive at reliable conclusions about what is real. Jesus participates in rational thinking without reducing Himself to abstract principles. The Good Samaritan (Luke 10:25–37) parable illustrates rational moral reasoning where assumptions are articulated and redefined regarding who constitutes a neighbor and what obligation there is to relieve suffering. Likewise, Jesus' teachings usually reveal supra-rational wisdom; reasoning regarding the ethical and relational logic exceeds any formulaic deduction (1 Corinthians 1:25). Jesus demonstrates that engaging rationalism is valid; however, relational and moral insight are more significant than deduction or simple calculation. Truth is not only coherent—truth is lived relationally and is historically witnessed (Barth 1936–1969; Kierkegaard 1843/1985).

Empiricism emphasizes knowledge acquired from sensory observation and evidence. Thomas' experience with the risen Christ (John 20:24–29) is illustrative of the tension between observation and belief. Jesus encourages Thomas to feel His wounds, affirming a convincing epistemology of the empirical, while simultaneously attesting that faith is valuable even where evidence cannot be experienced with the senses. Evidence exists in the form of witness accounts, historical records, and personal experiences, extending beyond empirical evidence alone. Empiricism is enriched when we consider the relational and historical context behind it, which suggests that a good, moral, ethical, or righteous declaration cannot be reduced to empirical data (Sanders 1993; McGrath 2010).

Pragmatism assesses truth based on utility and outcome. Healings, feeding the hungry, and serving were all actions in practice that served the immediate needs of human beings, but Jesus' call to discipleship—"Take up your cross daily" (Luke 9:23)—suggests that the end of the matter is not short-term success, but moral consequence and ethical responsibility. Like empiricism, pragmatism, when left to its own devices, becomes a shallow assumption of success, often reducing truth to expedience. Jesus demonstrates practical action informed by a transcendent ethical reality. He does not abandon usefulness, but ensures it is subordinated to moral and relational integrity (Taylor 2007; Smith 2014).

Scientism elevates observation, measurement, and natural law as the ultimate authority. Creation reveals a complexity of order and structure (Psalm 19; Romans 1:20), but science has limits, failing to deliver definitive solutions to questions of purpose, destiny, or moral obligation. Jesus represents Himself as the Truth (John 14:6), indicating that human experience and negotiation do not meet the measure of empiricism. While miracles and the resurrection

137

represent a reality beyond the natural laws observed by scientists, empirical observation has its limits in defining the human experience in its entirety. While science is valuable, it is not necessary to define human experience either individually or collectively (Polkinghorne 2001; McGrath 2010).

Nihilism demands a confrontation with human despair. Life is devoid of meaning. Ecclesiastes 1:2: "Vanity of vanities... all is vanity" articulates a profound sense of emptiness that echoes in modern nihilistic thought. Jesus enters that void with historical and relational presence. The cross looks like defeat but through resurrection, becomes the crucible of ultimate meaning, poignant evidence of hope and intentionality where nihilism only finds void (John 10:10). Jesus engages with existential despair, revealing that meaning, relational depth, and ethical coherence is not founded upon earthly success or measurable outcomes, but through historical and relational presence (Kierkegaard 1843/1985; Barth 1936-1969).

In this exchange, Jesus brings together the elements we have come to appreciate in modern philosophical paradigms while moving beyond their limitations. Rationality, observation, pragmatic outcome, and existential consciousness are all valued. Still, none of them become the basis for an individual's understanding of the totality. Identity, meaning, and moral action have cohered in a framework that is operational in historical and relational ethics. The reader is invited to engender modern intellectual and cultural constructs, without reductionism. Empirical, rational, pragmatic, and existential insights have value, and the framework of dialogue surrounding these elements is established within what is true about Christ's life, His teachings, and the historical witness (Lewis 1952; Wright 1996; Crossan 1991).

Identity in Christ as a Coherent Framework

In the current intellectual context, identity remains a contested arena for competing frameworks. Rationalism tends toward independent thought and logical coherence; empiricism privileges observation and what can be inferred from observable evidence; pragmatism considers selfhood in relation to utility or effectiveness; scientism locates importance in natural law and quantitative data; and nihilism observes the fragility and incompleteness of existence. Each of the previous perspectives offers meaningful insight into human life. Yet, no single perspective provides a coherent account of identity that is relational, moral, and historical in nature. Conversely, identity in Christ offers an integrative framework, bringing historical reality, relational fidelity, moral coherence, and significant transcendent ontological being into a living, observable practice (Barth 1936–1969; Kierkegaard 1843/1985; Lewis 1952).

Scripturally, the writings of Paul provide the basis for this formative, integrative understanding. Romans 8:29 reads, "For whom He foreknew, He also predestined to be conformed to the image of His Son, that He might be the firstborn among many brethren." In this text, identity is not merely an abstraction or a theoretical concept; rather, identity is a relational and moral formation characterized by historical reality. Importantly, the believer is formed in their self through being implicated in Christ's life, characterized by relational practices, ethical discernment, and moral coherence that conform to observable and quantitative factors in lived experience. Galatians 2:20 reinforces this, stating that one "lives by faith in the Son of God, who loved me and gave Himself for me." Identity is relationally enacted, meaning it emerges through one's interaction with others, as one navigates morally constructed choices and embodies grace, humility, and truth in specific contexts (Wright 1996; McGrath 2010).

This perspective acknowledges the limitations that exist in modern thought. In rationalism, for example, rationality might account for logical coherence, but it simply cannot define the ethical and relational self (Taylor 2007). Empiricism and scientism excel at observing the empirical world. Yet, they are unable to measure the relational depth, moral force, or ultimate purpose of anything (Polkinghorne 2001). Pragmatism provides practical evaluation, but pragmatism is based on the short-term and practical, thus cannot measure the lasting moral and spiritual reality (Smith 2014). Nihilism rightly recognizes the existential vulnerability of the self, but does not provide individuals with a fundamental coherence for anything we may call identity (Kierkegaard 1843; 1985). When the self is established in Christ, the above limitations, or challenges in modern thought, come together in coherence. Reason, observation, and pragmatic insight are employed, but in the context of a relational, ethical, and historically grounded reality.

The coherence of the self is practically evidenced first in observable behavior in life in Christ. The believer's life evidences relational fidelity—the ability to act with empathy, compassion, and moral fidelity in human relationships. Ethical discernment is reflected in choices that are consistent with the moral vision demonstrated in the life of Christ, characterized by justice, mercy, and humility. Grace shapes the experience of relationships by clarifying moral responsibility and fostering an understanding of moral failure. These elements of the self are not abstract ideals, nor simply aspirational. They are real and observable patterns of behavior, decision-making, and social interaction. In this sense, identity is both historical, as it is rooted in the concrete reality of Christ's life and witness; and morally coherent, as it provides a framework and continuity for an identity across different social and cultural contexts (Sanders 1993; Crossan 1991).

Integration is another important characteristic of the framework. Empirical observation, rational consideration, and pragmatic reasoning are not ignored, but rather integrated as ways to help navigate real existence effectively. Understanding trends in society, harnessing data, and resolving the complexities of ethical dilemmas—all of these are acceptable and necessary activities. However, our ultimate orientation is relational and ethically grounded, which ultimately exceeds being defined by metrics, abstraction, or even instrumental utility. Therefore, identity in Christ provides a coherent center that complexly integrates the observed, rational, and practical existence with a transcendent meaning and ethical coherence (Lewis 1952; Wright 1996).

Particularly in contemporary culture, where human identity is often fractured in the context of empirical data, social roles, or the influence of technology, the framework of Christ-centered identity provides a model for coherence. The self is not merely a collection of summaries of traits, observable outcomes, or empirically observable events; rather, the self is historically instantiated, ethically grounded, relational, and coherently and morally integrated. The believer's identity is a continuous, yet linear, process of participation in the life, teachings, and relational reality of Christ, shaping moral action, choices, and relationships over time and circumstance (Barth 1936–1969; McGrath 2010).

Within this framework, identity in Christ offers resistance to reductionism. It effectively integrates modern intellectual and cultural frameworks without falling apart into abstraction, utilitarian calculation, or nihilistic despair. Faith in Christ offers an immediate paradigm shift, moving from the historical to the moral, to help shape what it means to live authentically, morally, and relationally in the complexities of our modern lives.

Practical Applications for the 21st Century

In the present day, ethical engagement is no longer limited to abstract values or moral theories; rather, it is contextualized through the interchange between individual choice, social networks, and techno-environmental contexts. The contemporary environment is characterized by complexity in which rational reasoning, empirical observation, and pragmatic explanation intersect with cultural expectation, digital mediation, and rapid technological change. Here, the embodied realism of Jesus provides a pathway into these contexts without reducing human action to utility, measurement, or abstraction. Ethical engagement becomes a work of relational and historical discernment, where actions are situated within observable outcomes, historical memory, and moral responsibility (Barth 1936– 1969; Kierkegaard 1843/1985).

In the modern profession and organizational space, decisions made provide examples of this pattern. A manager, for example, who chooses to value transparency and integrity in a hiring, promotion, or collaboration context, is engaged in a framework of ethical action that is rooted in historical reality and relational accountability, reflecting the relational ethics of Christ's embodied life (Lewis 1952; Wright 1996). These choices help demonstrate that ethical engagement is observable and verifiable as it is committed to action; it is a move away from seeing action in terms of an abstract principle to observing the engagement as practice. Relational fidelity moves this ethical inquiry further into broader social and digital contexts. Communities, both physical and virtual, are saturated with competing metrics of value, influence, and performance. Social media platforms often quantify engagement, and professional networks may quantify success in numerical or transactional terms. A Christ-centered worldview alters relational engagement. Influence and connection become evaluative measurements, not simply in terms of how far or how efficiently, but in whether it is being done authentically, ethically, and with care for others (Smith, 2014). Abiding in Christ, as John 15:4–5 indicates, is not a personal endeavor of devotion, but a formative practice with real-world implications for our interactions. Relationships become contexts of moral inquiry and historical engagement, where decisions of influence and connection occur with empathy, accountability, and moral reflection, rather than superficial social calculation.

Negotiating the pressures of culture requires a sophisticated engagement with intellectual, technological, and moral awareness. Rationalism asserts that a settled thought is coherent, empiricism proves that ongoing observable events are happening, and pragmatism prioritizes the outcomes. However, those structures alone, when they are under severe attack, cannot be the grounding or the guide a person needs to shape their identity or guide their actions as they navigate cultural flux. The historical and relational reality of Christ provides an axis for stability - that identity is acted out ethically, in relation, and in history. Therefore, decisions are made through observation, reasoning, and practical epistemic wisdom, which provides ethical guidance based on a moral truth that has always existed (McGrath 2010; Polkinghorne 2001). It is in the technological spaces where this reasoning is most clearly seen. Artificial intelligence, data analytics, and algorithmic systems now provide unprecedented insight into human behavior and social patterns. However, those are only tools - telling us nothing about purpose, the need to understand relational significance, or moral urgency. Using these tools with discernment is not denying re-evaluating your focus. It needs to happen in a way that acknowledges the means without assuming that efficiency is meaningful, or that you can empirically ascertain the disposition or intentions to observe and comprehend the action in a moral sense, or that they understand the importance of relational fidelity.

Existential uncertainty pervades the modern age, underscoring the importance of coherence in action, identity, and moral reasoning. Nihilistic currents amplify what we know to be true and observable, while not knowing or living with significance represents fragility, loss, and the impermanent qualities that are real - Christ's life, death, and resurrection model construct as a relational and historical axis for settling in identity and addressing the void, but not ignoring realities (Kierkegaard 1843/1985; Ecclesiastes 1:2). Now, decisions can view the process through a lens that binds history, ethics, and relational goodwill to inform action with confidence. Culture, technological changes, and social pressures will all interact with the pressures of an ethical responsibility. But a connection will emerge if we act coherently as a people bound and ordered by our history, relational trust, and moral reality (Taylor 2007; Sanders 1993).

Reflection becomes, in its own right, a tool for a way of being that engages propagation. Reflecting on actions, relationships, and decisions through the lens of Christ's historical reality is a formative experience. It cultivates good engagement in working to understand how the individual perceives reality, reasons in their thought process, calculates outcomes, and takes responsibility for ethics. In the most routine engagements of daily life, such as in families, workplaces, communities, and cyberspaces, we reflect on each of these categories to see coherence in our understanding of identity. Thus, action is not simply abstract or reduced to utility; the observable and historical realities interact as a witness to moral persuasion, purpose, and a sense of moral ire with human action, observed through an observable relationship (Crossan 1991; Wright 1996).

Living ethically and relationally in the twenty-first century is an ongoing negotiation of the complexities we have today, in the historic and relational context of Christ's reality. The decisions, interactions, and engagement are not an end in themselves, but are an articulation of identity, bounded by the past, with messy relational dedication, moral reasoning, and ethical engagement informing the decisions. Practical application will not come through formula or prescription, but through ongoing, reflective, and experienced engagement with identity, meaning, and action within the concrete realities of the world we live in today (Barth 1936–1969; McGrath 2010).

The Upside-Down Kingdom and Moral Orientation

The Gospels portray a kingdom established by Jesus that is counterintuitive in expectation and worldly calculus. The Beatitudes (Matthew 5) are a clear depiction: the poor in spirit, the meek, and the persecuted—specifically those whom the world counts as powerless or of no value—are called blessed. This "upside-down" arrangement of reality disrupts competing questions about whether power, wealth, visibility, or observable success mean ultimate significance. To live in light of this kingdom means reordering moral and relational priorities and situating human agency in a manner that is both observable in history and transcendent (Barth 1936–1969; Kierkegaard 1843/1985).

Worldviews that are "of the earth" can all be measured in varying terms of success by the consequences of outcomes, efficiency, and measurable achievement. Rationalism values coherence or reasoning, pragmatism balances with utility, and empiricism privileges observation. Yet, none honor the relational, ethical, and historical dimensions of reality that Jesus embodies in his ministry. Jesus illustrates that moral authority is never limited to utility, predictability, or observable consequence by healing the sick, engaging with the disenfranchised, and teaching through parable (Lewis 1952; Wright 1996). The upside-down kingdom requires adopting a kind of responsibility that involves an ethical and relational orientation before pursuing instrumental outcomes. A teacher who corrects with patience, a manager who prioritizes integrity over expediency, or a friend who prioritizes care over comfort all embody kingdom ethics and cannot be fully understood by worldly outcomes.

This kingdom orientation creates a unique disorientation when navigating between the observable world and transcendent consequences. Actions and decisions occur simultaneously, but in different temporal domains, such as work, community, or social networks, as well as in a broader ethical and moral context, as demonstrated by Christ. To address systemic injustice, one must examine not only the long-standing patterns of injustice but also the practical implications of the response, as well as the social dynamics at play (or not). The action guide is not judged by its current effectiveness or social capital, but rather by its consistency with moral fidelity and integrity. In the upside-down kingdom, we must redefine success; what may be small, weak, or inconvenient in worldly terms could hold lasting significance (Taylor 2007; Sanders 1993).

To live ethically in the kingdom means recognizing both limits and possibilities. We have succinct examples in the epistemologies of scientism and nihilism that reveal the precariousness of observable metrics and the continual potential for despair; yet, the ministry of Jesus inserts human action into a historically real and relationally grounded purpose. The cross is the ultimate example of this principle: that which appears to be defeat and humiliation is the source of ultimate meaningfulness. Ethical and moral action is never separated from historical reality, or any semblance of the transcendent (Ecclesiastes 1:2; John 10:10; Kierkegaard 1843/1985). In this way, the kingdom provides focus in a world grappling with cultural influences, technological advancement, and existential uncertainty. Ethical discernment and relational fidelity are practices that imbue day-to-day decision-making with lasting significance, bridging the observable and the transcendent.

Of particular interest, the Beatitudes mate social, ethical, and moral processes in complex ways. The poor in spirit model humility in the face of intellectual pride; the mourners model empathy and recognition of suffering; the meek model restraint and moral patience in contexts of conflict or competition; the hungry and thirsty for righteousness persistently sustain ethical reflection and engagement (Barth 1936-1969; Smith 2014). These are not moral abstractions but rather dispositions grounded in action, historical reality, and relational practices. The dispositions serve as a bridge for believers in the ongoing striving through the complexity of modern existence, a part of which is reductionism, nihilistic despair, and ethical capitulation.

The upside-down kingdom offers a lens into the intersection of identity, meaning, and action. Meaningfulness, within this framework, is not defined by immediate visibility, measurable success, or social approval, but by the embodiment of Christ's historical and relational realities. Ethical and relational orientations become concrete expressions of identity, grounded in moral coherence, historical witness, and relational significance. This perspective provides moral clarity in a world shaped by accumulated empirical data, rational accounting, and technological influence.

Human action is meaningful when it reflects lasting truth, relational accountability, and a historic ethical vision (Crossan 1991; Wright 1996).

Coherent Living in a Complex World

In today's world, we find ourselves in a context filled with rival frameworks for making sense of reality. Rationalism seeks coherence in thinking; empiricism values attending to what observation reveals, observing, and the evidence that can be presented; pragmatism attends to usefulness; scientism honors measurement; nihilism seeks to disclose the tenuousness of making sense. Each framework offers important insights into why and how we exist as we do, but none contain the fullness of who we are as human beings, alongside moral agency and the depth of our relations. In this context, the historical and relational reality of Christ attends to the partial truths of these frameworks without reducing them, allowing us to make sense of how identity, meaning, and action cohere in complex contexts (Barth, 1936-1969; Tillich, 1951; Taylor, 2007).

Identity in Christ is neither abstract nor separate. As Paul puts it, "We are being conformed to the image of His Son" (Rom 8:29), as we engage in this process within history, in our relationships, and in our moral practices. The Gospels and letters depict life situated in the flesh and blood reality, marked by hunger and fatigue, dialogue and teaching, suffering and resurrection. Embodied realism grounds moral discernment and relational fidelity by reminding us that identity is not simply grounded in thought, observation, or usefulness - identity is, quite simply, participation in a coherent historical and moral reality (Kierkegaard 1844/1985; Wright 1996). Identity lived out publicly is identifiable in the decisions, actions, and interactions that call us to moral recognition and relational responsibility. Lived identity is observable, accountable, and formative.

Meaning is, similarly, yoked to relational and historical context. Modern philosophies frequently endeavor to derive meaning from abstract ideas, data, or computation. In contrast, the Gospel situates meaning within the context of human experience and divine involvement. The cross, the resurrection, and Jesus' ministry convey a reality in which what seems weak, marginal, or paradoxical according to the ways of the world serves as a basis for ultimate meaning. Nihilistic despair is addressed not with an indictment of reality but with orienting suffering, limitation, and uncertainty toward ultimate significance (Ecclesiastes 1:2; Lewis 1952). In Christ, relational and ethical coherence transforms chaos and contingency into a framework where choices, relationships, and activities take on enduring meaning (Tillich 1951; McGrath 2007).

Action in the modern world is inherently multi-layered. Technological acceleration, cultural pluralism, and social fragmentation necessitate discernment that honors the engagement of observation, reasoning, and practical consequence. Yet, these tools are not sufficient on their own. Christ-centered realism engages empirical and rational observations, embedding them within a relational and ethical framework (Polkinghorne 2007; Smith 2014). Choices made as professionals, citizens, or participants in a digital world are assessed not only in terms of efficiency or visibility but also in relation to moral groundedness, historical possibility, and relational loyalty. The wisdom of Christ offers a guiding principle for navigating ethical dilemmas, personal relationships, and societal pressures, providing an alternative to reductionism and nihilistic despair.

This developed coherence extends into the community and society. Ethical and relational living in both observable and transcendent space spiritually engages interactions in family, work, civic organization, and digital society. Grace, humility, and fidelity become more than concepts; they become observable practices that hold relational networks together, build trust, and orient collective life toward enduring good. Identity, meaning, and action intersect dynamically: ethical behavior emerges from a coherent identity, relational engagement informs moral discernment, and historical understanding situates both in time and world. The Christ-centered framework argues that living realistically does not require abandoning purpose or moral clarity, but rather cultivates awareness of options, coherence, and resilience within and across the multiple layers of modern life (Barth, 1936–1969; Wright, 1996; Taylor, 2007).

Ultimately, the Gospel provides a framework for coherent living that neither assumes a rejection of modern understanding nor succumbs to reductionistic philosophies. Rationalism, empiricism, pragmatism, scientism, and nihilism all offer partial glimpses into reality. Yet, the life, death, and resurrection of Jesus demonstrate how these glimpses are fully realized, grounded, and lived out ethically. The reader is invited not merely to accept dogmatic assertions about Jesus but to engage with what it means to live within a living framework in which identity, meaning, and activity cannot be separated and where historical practices, observation, and ethical considerations shape moral and relational understandings. In Christ, the way forward through the complexities, uncertainties, and frequently fractured modern world is intellectually engaging, a reality that is coherent and purposeful (Lewis, 1952; Crossan, 1991; McGrath, 2007).

As we close this journey, the reader is invited to step into a reality where faith, reason, observation, and action are not in competition but in dialogue. Across the challenges of rationalism, empiricism, pragmatism, scientism, and nihilism, Jesus emerges as both historically grounded and relationally present, offering a framework for identity, meaning, and ethical action that coheres across time and culture. To live realistically in Christ is to embrace a life informed by evidence, guided by reason, oriented toward practical engagement, and rooted in enduring moral and relational truths. In this upside-down kingdom, ultimate significance is measured not by worldly success or immediate visibility, but by fidelity to a historical, ethical, and relational reality that transforms both individual lives and the communities in which they move. The invitation is clear: to navigate the complexities, uncertainties, and wonders of the modern world not by abstraction or despair, but through participation in a life that is coherent, purposeful, and deeply human, as revealed in Christ.

References / Bibliography

Aquinas, Thomas. 1947. Summa Theologica. Translated by Fathers of the English Dominican Province. London: Burns, Oates & Washbourne.Barth, Karl. 1936. Church Dogmatics. Zurich: Theologischer Verlag Zürich.Barth, Karl. 1936. Church Dogmatics: Volume III/3: The Doctrine of Creation. Edinburgh: T&T Clark.

Barth, Karl. 1967. Church Dogmatics. Edinburgh: T&T Clark.

Bhaskar, Roy. 1978. A Realist Theory of Science. Brighton: Harvester Press.

Bhaskar, Roy. 1978. A Realist Theory of Science. Leeds: Leeds Books.

Craig, William Lane. 2008. Reasonable Faith: Christian Truth and Apologetics. 3rd ed. Wheaton, IL: Crossway.

Crossan, John Dominic. 1991. The Historical Jesus: The Life of a Mediterranean Jewish Peasant. San Francisco: HarperSanFrancisco.

Descartes, René. 1641. Meditations on First Philosophy. Paris: Michel de Sol.

Hume, David. 1748. An Enquiry Concerning Human Understanding. London: A. Millar.

John. 1996. Holy Bible. Nashville, TN: Thomas Nelson.

Kierkegaard, Søren. 1983. Fear and Trembling and The Concept of Anxiety. Princeton, NJ: Princeton University Press.

Lewis, C. S. 1943. The Abolition of Man. New York: Macmillan.

Lewis, C. S. 1947. The Abolition of Man. London: Oxford University Press.

Lewis, C. S. 1952. Mere Christianity. London: Geoffrey Bles.

Lewis, C. S. 1952. Mere Christianity. New York: Macmillan.

MacIntyre, Alasdair. 1981. After Virtue: A Study in Moral Theory. Notre Dame, IN: University of Notre Dame Press.

McGrath, Alister E. 2000. Science & Religion: An Introduction. Oxford: Blackwell Publishers.

Nietzsche, Friedrich. 1883. Thus Spoke Zarathustra. Chemnitz: Ernst Schmeitzner.

Pascal, Blaise. 1966. Pensées. Translated by W. F. Trotter. New York: Macmillan.

Pascal, Blaise. 1966. Pensées. Translated by W.F. Trotter. London: Dent.

Polkinghorne, John. 2001. Science and Providence: God's Interaction with the World. London: SPCK.

Polkinghorne, John. 2005. Science and Providence: God's Interaction with the World. London: SPCK.

Putnam, Hilary. 1975. Mathematics, Matter, and Method. Cambridge: Cambridge University Press.

Putnam, Hilary. 1975. Mathematics, Matter, and Method: Philosophical Papers, Volume 1. Cambridge: Cambridge University Press.

Sanders, E. P. 1993. The Historical Figure of Jesus. London: Penguin.

Smith, James K. A. 2014. How (Not) to Be Secular: Reading Charles Taylor. Grand Rapids, MI: Eerdmans.

Spinoza, Baruch. 1677. Ethics. Amsterdam: Jan Rieuwertsz.

Spinoza, Benedictus de. 1677. Ethics. Amsterdam: Jan Rieuwertsz.

Taylor, Charles. 2007. A Secular Age. Cambridge, MA: Belknap Press of Harvard University Press.

Tillich, Paul. 1967. Systematic Theology. Chicago: University of Chicago Press.

Vermes, Geza. 1973. Jesus the Jew: A Historian's Reading of the Gospels. London: Collins.

Wright, N. T. 1996. Jesus and the Victory of God. Minneapolis, MN: Fortress Press.

Wright, N. T. 2003. The *Resurrection of the Son of God*. Minneapolis: Fortress Press.